War in the West
Pea Ridge and Prairie Grove

CIVIL WAR CAMPAIGNS AND COMMANDERS SERIES

Under the General Editorship of Grady McWhiney

PUBLISHED

War in the West
Pea Ridge and Prairie Grove

William L. Shea

Under the General Editorship of Grady McWhiney

RYAN PLACE PUBLISHERS
FORT WORTH   BOULDER

Cataloging-in-Publication Data

Shea, William L.
    War in the west: Pea Ridge and Prairie Grove / William L. Shea.
      p. cm. – (Civil War campaigns and commanders)
    Includes bibliographical references (p.   ) and index.
    ISBN 1-886661-14-6 (pbk)

    1. Pea Ridge, Battle of, 1862. 2. Prairie Grove, Battle of, 1862.
    I. Title. II. Series

    E473.77.S545 1996
    973.7'32—dc20   96–24827
                                                CIP

Copyright © 1996, Ryan Place Publishers, Inc.

2730 Fifth Avenue
Fort Worth, Texas 76110

Printed in the United States of America

ISBN 1-886661-14-6
10 9 8 7 6 5 4 3 2 1

Book Designed by Rosenbohm Design Group

All inquiries regarding volume purchases of this book should be
addressed to Ryan Place Publishers, Inc., 2525 Arapahoe Avenue,
Suite E4-231, Boulder, CO 80302-6720.

SAN: 298-6779

A NOTE ON THE SERIES

Few segments of America's past excite more interest than Civil War battles and leaders. This ongoing series of brief, lively, and authoritative books–*Civil War Campaigns and Commanders*–salutes this passion with inexpensive and accurate accounts that are readable in a sitting. Each volume, separate and complete in itself, nevertheless conveys the agony, glory, death, and wreckage that defined America's greatest tragedy.

In this series, designed for Civil War enthusiasts as well as the newly recruited, emphasis is on telling good stories. Photographs and biographical sketches enhance the narrative of each book, and maps depict events as they happened. Sound history is meshed with the dramatic in a format that is just lengthy enough to inform and yet satisfy.

Grady McWhiney
General Editor

CONTENTS

The brief biographies accompanying the photographs
were written by Grady McWhiney and David Coffey.

CAMPAIGNS AND COMMANDERS SERIES

Map Key

Geography

	Trees
	Marsh
	Fields
	Strategic Elevations
	Rivers
	Tactical Elevations
)|(	Fords
	Orchards
— — — —	Political Boundaries

Human Construction

	Bridges
+++++++	Railroads
	Tactical Towns
● ○	Strategic Towns
□ ■	Buildings
†	Church
✕	Roads

Military

 Union Infantry

Confederate Infantry

 Cavalry

ılı Artillery

 Headquarters

 Encampments

 Fortifications

Permanant Works

 Hasty Works

Obstructions

Engagements

Warships

Gunboats

Casemate Ironclad

Monitor

Tactical Movements

Strategic Movements

Maps by
Donald S. Frazier, Ph.D.
Abilene, Texas

MAPS

PHOTOGRAPHS AND ILLUSTRATIONS

War in the West
Pea Ridge and Prairie Grove

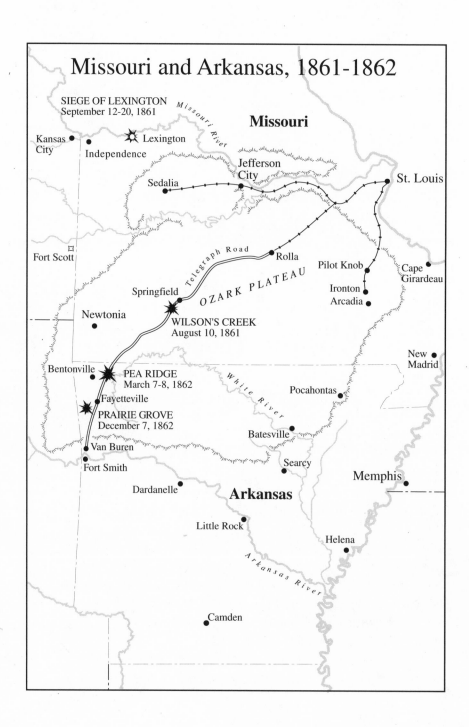

Missouri and Arkansas, 1861-1862

SIEGE OF LEXINGTON
September 12-20, 1861

Missouri River

Missouri

Kansas City

Independence

Lexington

Sedalia

Jefferson City

St. Louis

Fort Scott

Telegraph Road

Rolla

Pilot Knob

Cape Girardeau

OZARK PLATEAU

Springfield

Ironton

Arcadia

Newtonia

WILSON'S CREEK
August 10, 1861

Bentonville

White River

New Madrid

Pocahontas

PEA RIDGE
March 7-8, 1862

Fayetteville

PRAIRIE GROVE
December 7, 1862

Batesville

Van Buren

Fort Smith

Searcy

Memphis

Dardanelle

Arkansas

Little Rock

Helena

Arkansas River

Camden

1
BEYOND THE MISSISSIPPI

The first year of the Civil War in Missouri did not go particularly well for the Confederacy. Missouri was a slave state, but only a small proportion of the state's population owned slaves or approved of secession. Though heavily outnumbered, pro-secessionist forces had the initial advantage of dominating the Missouri State Guard—the state militia—which was commanded by a popular former governor named Sterling Price. During the spring of 1861 the Missouri State Guard struggled against rapidly expanding Union forces for control of the state's population centers and its political institutions. After a confused series of marches, countermarches, and small clashes, Price and his men were pushed into the southwestern corner of Missouri. By midsummer Union forces appeared to be on the verge of a complete victory.

The Union commander in Missouri was Brigadier General Nathaniel Lyon, a fiery regular soldier who was determined to rid the state of the troublesome Rebels once and for all. In July he advanced into southwestern Missouri toward Price's "capital" at Springfield. Price called upon Brigadier General Benjamin McCulloch, who commanded a Confederate army in

Sterling Price: born Virginia 1809; attended Hampden-Sydney College and studied law; moved with his family to Missouri in 1830; served in the state legislature and in 1844 was elected to the U.S. House of Representatives; resigned from Congress to lead a regiment of Missouri troops in the Mexican War; promoted to brigadier general of volunteers in 1848; governor of Missouri from 1853 to 1857; he was president of the Missouri convention that voted against secession, but a dispute with radicals prompted his break from the Unionist ranks; offered his services to secessionist Governor C.F. Jackson and accepted command of the Missouri state militia; worked to maintain peace in Missouri, but after negotiations with Union leaders broke down in June 1861, he prepared his troops to oppose

Federal forces; combined with General Ben McCulloch's Confederate troops to defeat the Federals at Wilson's Creek, Missouri, in August 1861; captured Lexington, Missouri, in September before retreating into Arkansas; led Missouri troops in General Earl Van Dorn's Confederate force at Elkhorn Tavern, Arkansas, in March 1862; following that defeat, the Missouri troops were mustered into Confederate service and Price was commissioned major general; transferred to Mississippi despite his fervent protest; suffered defeats at Iuka and Corinth before returning to Arkansas; defeated at Helena in 1863; supported General E. Kirby Smith in repulsing General Frederick Steele's Arkansas portion of the Red River Campaign in the spring of 1864; that fall he led an ambitious cavalry raid into Missouri, but after initial success, was turned back in eastern Kansas; retreating through Indian Territory and northern Texas, Price's remnant returned to Arkansas in December; at the close of the war Price refused to surrender and escaped to Mexico; upon the collapse of Maximilian's empire in 1866, Price returned to Missouri, where he died the following year. Called "Old Pap" by his men, Price was a devoted soldier. While his 1864 raid and subsequent exodus to Mexico have been highly romanticized, his overall military performance was largely unimpressive.

northwestern Arkansas, for help. McCulloch's mission was to defend Arkansas and the Indian Territory (present-day Oklahoma) from a Union invasion. His instructions were to remain on the defensive on Confederate soil, but he recognized that Price's Missouri State Guard played an important strategic role: it kept Missouri in turmoil and served as a buffer

Benjamin McCulloch: born Tennessee 1811; McCulloch followed his friend and neighbor David Crockett to Texas in 1835; unable to reach San Antonio before the fall of the Alamo, he served under Sam Houston in the Battle of San Jacinto; remaining in Texas, he worked as a surveyor and embarked on a brilliant career as a Texas Ranger, Indian fighter, and scout; in 1839 he was elected to the Republic of Texas House of Representatives but served only one two-year term; he served

with great distinction under Zachary Taylor during the Mexican War and gained a national reputation as commander of a Ranger company and Taylor's chief of scouts; during the 1849 Gold Rush, McCulloch ventured to California; failing to find his fortune, he returned to Texas; he was considered for the colonelcy of the newly constituted 2d U.S. Cavalry, the command of which went to his fellow Texan Albert Sidney Johnston; in 1854 he became a U.S. marshal in Texas and in 1858 helped negotiate a settlement between the Mormon's and the federal government; with the secession of Texas, McCulloch became a colonel of Texas state troops and secured the surrender of the Federal garrison at San Antonio; in May 1861 he was commissioned a brigadier general in the Confederate army and

given command of the Indian Territory; assigned to command Confederate troops in Arkansas, he defeated General Nathaniel Lyon's Federal forces at Wilson's Creek, Missouri, in August 1861; a continuing feud with Missouri General Sterling Price forced the Confederate government to place McCulloch and Price under the command of General Earl Van Dorn; General McCulloch was killed while commanding the right wing in the Battle of Pea Ridge in March 1862; his death was considered a major blow to Confederate aspirations in the Trans-Mississippi; his brother, Henry E. McCulloch, also served the Confederacy as a brigadier general.

between Union forces and his own Confederate army in Arkansas. McCulloch therefore edged across the state line to reinforce Price in his hour of need.

Lyon was undeterrred by news of McCulloch's movement into southwestern Missouri. He recklessly attacked the combined Missouri State Guard and Confederate armies at Wilson's Creek, just south of Springfield, on August 10, 1861. The ensuing battle was a disaster for the Union cause. Lyon was killed and his little army was driven from the field. McCulloch was pleased at the hard-fought victory but he was exasperated by Price, whom he privately disparaged as "nothing but an old militia general." McCulloch also was uneasy at having invaded Missouri without orders from the Confederate government, and he soon returned to Arkansas. (The United States was, after all, a foreign country from the Confederate perspective.)

Price, in contrast to McCulloch, was a free agent who was not bound by orders from the Confederate government in far-away Virginia. He was far more of a politician than a soldier, and he saw the war entirely in terms of liberating his constituents in Missouri from Yankee oppression. "Old Pap," as he was known to his men, was exhilarated by the outcome of Wilson's Creek and immediately marched north to the Missouri River hoping to ignite a widespread popular uprising. On September 20 Price captured a small Union garrison at Lexington and threw a fright into Unionists from Kansas City to St. Louis, but the expected popular support failed to materialize. To make matters worse, Price soon discovered that he could not sustain his command so far north and fell back to the Springfield area.

During the fall Major General John C. Fremont assembled another Union army and made a second attempt to drive Price from Missouri, but he was relieved in mid-campaign by President Abraham Lincoln who had become displeased with Fremont's political machinations and lack of administrative ability. In November a rump session of the Missouri legislature met near Springfield and declared the state to be a part of the Confederacy. The legitimacy of this act was dubious, to say the least, but it was accepted by Confederate authorities in Virginia and another star was added to the Confederate flag.

During the winter of 1861-62 the military stalemate in Missouri continued. Union forces dominated the central and northern portions of the state, while the Confederates defiantly stood their ground in the southwestern corner. Price's ragtag army consisted of about 8,000 men and 47 cannon. The army was seriously deficient in organization, training, and logistical support. Volunteers provided their own weapons, clothing, and camp equipment. Despite their distinctly unmilitary appearance, many of the soldiers were veterans of Wilson's Creek, Lexington, and other small engagements in Missouri. At this stage of the war Price's army was an anomalous mix of Missouri State Guardsmen and newly enrolled Confederate soldiers. Price himself remained a Missouri State Guard major general; he would not receive his Confederate commission as a major general until after Pea Ridge. The force was scattered in and around Springfield, huddled in makeshift shelters against the winter storms that regularly swept across the Ozark Plateau.

McCulloch's Confederate army was located in northwestern Arkansas about one hundred miles south of Price's force. McCulloch was a respected former Texas Ranger and Mexican War veteran. His small but well drilled command consisted of 8,700 men and 18 cannon. Many of his Arkansas, Louisiana, and Texas soldiers were veterans of Wilson's Creek and other engagements in Missouri and the Indian Territory. The infantry was in winter quarters in and around Fayetteville, Bentonville, and Cross Hollows, enduring the frigid weather; the cavalry and artillery were spread out along the Arkansas River Valley sixty miles to the south, where warmer temperatures and adequate forage for horses and mules made life more bearable for man and beast.

McCulloch did not expect any military activity atop the Ozark Plateau until spring, so he traveled to Virginia to confer with Confederate President Jefferson Davis about the state of affairs in the Trans-Mississippi. McCulloch wanted to discuss his long-simmering feud with Price, which had begun after Wilson's Creek when Price wanted to push north to the Missouri River and McCulloch wanted to fall back into Arkansas. After several months of increasingly bitter wrangling the two generals no longer were on speaking terms. Davis resolved the impasse with the stroke of a pen by creating the District of the Trans-Mississippi, a vast area consisting of Missouri, Arkansas, northern Louisiana, and the Indian Territory, and placing Major General Earl Van Dorn in overall

Earl Van Dorn: born Mississippi 1820; Van Dorn was graduated from the U.S. Military Academy in 1842, fifty-second in his class of fifty-six; a brevet second lieutenant, he was posted to the 7th Infantry; he owned an exceptionally active career, serving in various garrison and frontier commands; twice brevetted for the

Mexican War, he was promoted to first lieutenant in 1847 and served against the Seminoles in Florida; in 1855 Van Dorn became a captain in the newly organized 2d U.S. Cavalry, an elite regiment that included Albert Sidney Johnston, Robert E. Lee, George H. Thomas, William J. Hardee, and John B. Hood; in Texas he fought numerous actions against the Comanches and was wounded in an engagement in Indian Territory; with Mississippi's withdrawal from the Union in 1860, Van Dorn, having been promoted to major, tendered his resignation to serve his native state; he became a brigadier general of Mississippi state troops and rose to major general commanding state troops upon Jefferson Davis's election as president of the Confederate States; entering Confederate service in March 1861, Van Dorn was commissioned a colonel and briefly commanded Forts Jackson and St. Philip that guarded the

command. Davis believed that the new arrangement would provide unity of command and purpose to the disorganized Confederate war effort west of the Mississippi River.

Van Dorn was a professional soldier with years of experience fighting Indians on the Great Plains, but he proved to be a poor choice for such an important assignment. He was impulsive, reckless, and lacking in administrative skills. None of these flaws were apparent, however, as Van Dorn hastened westward from Virginia to his new post. The new commander was intensely offensive-minded. He intended to liberate Missouri—now nominally a Confederate state—at the first opportunity. Van Dorn established his headquarters in Pocahontas in the northeastern part of Arkansas because he

southern approaches to New Orleans; he was soon appointed commander of the Department of Texas, where his performance earned him promotion to brigadier general in June 1861; ordered to Virginia, he was elevated to major general and commanded a division under General Joseph E. Johnston; returned to the West in January 1862, he commanded the Trans-Mississippi District of Department Number Two and the small Army of the West; that March he was defeated at the Battle of Pea Ridge; he then led his army across the Mississippi to reinforce General P.G.T. Beauregard's beleaguered force at Corinth, Mississippi; given command of the Department of Southern Mississippi and East Louisiana, he worked to defend Vicksburg, but his harsh administration of the department led to his removal in July 1862; after being soundly defeated at Corinth in October, he assumed command of the cavalry under his successor in Mississippi, General John C. Pemberton; much better suited for a cavalry command, Van Dorn turned in his finest Civil War performance with his December 1862 raid on General U.S. Grant's Holly Springs depot; in addition to destroying tons of Federal supplies, the raid delayed Grant's advance on Vicksburg; Van Dorn then headed a cavalry division in General Braxton Bragg's Army of Tennessee and was successful in several clashes in central Tennessee; a handsome and dashing figure, Van Dorn, although married, was a known ladies' man, whose transgressions often drew the consternation of fellow officers and citizens alike; while headquartered at Spring Hill, Tennessee, he spent much time with the young wife of a local physician; in May 1863 the aggrieved husband, Dr. James Peters, confronted Van Dorn in the general's quarters and shot him to death.

planned to march north from that point in the spring. Van Dorn expressed his rather casual approach to strategy in a letter to his wife: "I must have St. Louis—then Huzza!"

Meanwhile, Lincoln tried to solve his own problems west of

Samuel R. Curtis: born New York 1805; at a young age Curtis removed with his family to Ohio; he was graduated from the U.S. Military Academy in 1831, twenty-seventh in his class of thirty-three; commissioned brevet 2d lieutenant and posted to infantry, Curtis resigned after one year's service in the Indian Territory; returning to Ohio, he worked as a civil engineer and studied law; long active in the state militia, he was adjutant general of Ohio at the outbreak of the Mexican War, but soon became colonel of the 2d Ohio Volunteers, serving competently under General Zachary Taylor in Mexico; after the war he continued his engineering endeavors; in the mid-1850s Curtis relocated to Keokuk, Iowa, where he opened a law practice; in 1856 he was elected mayor of Keokuk and, later that year, to the U.S. House of

Representatives; during his third term, in 1861, Curtis resigned his seat to enter the U.S. Volunteers as colonel of the 2d Iowa Infantry; appointed brigadier general of volunteers in May 1861, Curtis commanded the victorious Federal forces in the Battle of Pea Ridge, Arkansas, the following spring; promoted to major general, U.S.V., he continued to perform well in the isolated Trans-Mississippi; in the summer of 1862 his forces captured Helena, Arkansas, after which he became commander of the Department of Missouri; a conflict between Curtis and Missouri Governor William Gamble forced President Abraham Lincoln to remove the general in the spring of 1863; thereafter, Curtis assumed command of the Department of Kansas and shared in the repulse of Confederate General Sterling Price's 1864 Raid; from February to July 1865 Curtis commanded the Department of the Northwest, and soon thereafter represented the Army in treaty negotiations with several tribes of Northern Plains Indians; his last service came as an examiner on the construction of the Union Pacific Railroad; mustered out of the volunteer army in April 1866, General Curtis died that December at Council Bluffs, Iowa; he remains among the more underappreciated contributors to the Federal war effort.

the Mississippi River by appointing Major General Henry W. Halleck to succeed Fremont as commander of the Department of the Missouri. Halleck was an able administrator and strategist who was determined to reassert Union control over all of Missouri. He understood that every Federal soldier standing on the defensive in Missouri to counter Price was one less soldier who could be used in the offensive campaigns he planned to launch on the Tennessee, Cumberland, and Mississippi Rivers in the near future. Halleck believed it was imperative that Union forces neutralize Price immediately rather than wait for more suitable weather in the spring. On Christmas Day, 1861, he placed Brigadier General Samuel R. Curtis in command of the Army of the Southwest, a force of about 12,000 men and fifty cannon. Curtis's mission was urgent and straightforward: he was to destroy Price's army or drive it out of Missouri.

Curtis was a successful engineer, businessman, and politician who proved to be a surprisingly able and aggressive soldier. He hurried to the railhead at Rolla and began to prepare for the coming offensive. He had no illusions about the difficulty of a winter campaign atop the Ozark Plateau. The vast limestone uplift occupied the southern half of Missouri and the northern half of Arkansas, and was one of the most rugged and sparsely settled regions in the country. To complicate matters, every step toward Springfield would take Curtis farther away from his logistical base at Rolla. Union armies in Virginia and Tennessee were largely transported and supplied by steamboats and trains, but in Missouri there were few navigable rivers and even fewer railroads. Atop the Ozark Plateau there were none at all. The Army of the Southwest and its supply wagons would have to proceed along primitive frontier roads. Curtis ruthlessly stripped his command of useless baggage, for he realized that the Union troops would have to travel light and forage vigorously. He requested an experienced quartermaster from the regular army and obtained one in the person of

Captain Phillip H. Sheridan, who would later go on to greater things.

Halleck was painfully aware of the seesaw nature of the war in Missouri up to that point. Every Union setback had encouraged the secessionists and demoralized the loyalists.

Philip Henry Sheridan: born New York 1831; Sheridan's date and place of birth remain matters of speculation; Sheridan himself gave conflicting information; he may have been born in Ireland or aboard ship during his Irish parents' passage to the United States; whatever the case, the family moved to Ohio when Sheridan was still an infant; he entered the U.S. Military Academy with the class of 1852, but disciplinary problems delayed his graduation by a year; he finished thirty-fourth in the 1853 class of fifty-two that included John Bell Hood, James B. McPherson, and John M. Schofield; after years of service on the frontier with the 4th Infantry, Sheridan was still a 2d lieutenant on the eve of the Civil War; promoted to 1st lieutenant in March 1861 and captain, 13th Infantry, in May, he served as chief quartermaster and commissary for the Army of Southwest Missouri and was detailed to General Henry Halleck's headquarters during the advance on Corinth, Mississippi; in May 1862 he entered the volunteer army as colonel of the 2d Michigan Cavalry and, by July, was promoted to brigadier general, U.S. Volunteers; he commanded an infantry division at Perryville and Stone's River, gaining promotion to major general, U.S. Volunteers, to date from December 1862; Sheridan's division was routed at Chickamauga in September 1863, but spearheaded the unauthorized assault that drove the Confederates from Missionary Ridge in November; when General Ulysses S. Grant was named overall commander of Union forces and went east to face General Robert E. Lee, he selected Sheridan to lead the Army of the Potomac's Cavalry Corps; throughout the spring and early summer of 1864, Sheridan's troopers duelled with the once-supreme Rebel cavalry with mixed results; he was victorious in the clash at Yellow

Another unsuccessful campaign would have repercussions far outside Missouri by delaying vital operations along the Confederacy's vulnerable western waterways. "We must have no failure in this movement against Price," he cautioned Curtis. "It must be the last."

Tavern, in which Confederate cavalry commander J.E.B. Stuart was mortally wounded; in response to Confederate General Jubal Early's move on Washington, Grant created the Middle Military Division and placed Sheridan in command; Sheridan's Army of the Shenandoah, consisting of two infantry corps and three large divisions of cavalry, defeated Early at Winchester and Fisher's Hill but narrowly escaped disaster at Cedar Creek when the Rebels surprised Sheridan's army during his absence; Sheridan's ride from Winchester to Cedar Creek to rally his men is among the most well-publicized events of the war; during the fall and winter of 1864-1865, in an awesome display of total war, Sheridan's troops laid waste to the Shenadoah Valley, depriving Lee of much-needed supplies and incurring the wrath of Southerners for generations to come; the fiery Sheridan became a national hero; having been promoted to brigadier general in the regular army in September 1864, he became major general in November; in the spring of 1865 Sheridan, with the bulk of his command, rejoined Grant on the Petersburg front and played a pivotal role in the closing stages of the war; given wide discretion, Sheridan's cavalry ran roughshod over the Rebels at Five Forks and Sayler's Creek, finally cornering Lee's army near Appomattox; while extremely successful on the battlefield, Sheridan's abrasive manner and quick temper led to the unfair removal of General G.K. Warren, a controversy that raged for years; immediately after Lee's surrender, Sheridan was dispatched to the south Texas border with Mexico to discourage French intentions in that country; thereafter his heavy-handed conduct as the reconstruction commander of the Fifth Military District (Texas and Louisiana) brought his removal; when Grant became president and William T. Sherman filled his spot as commanding general, Sheridan became lieutenant general; as commander of the Military Division of the Missouri, he was an aggressive prosecutor of the Indian Wars; during this period he was also an official observer of the Franco-Prussian War and supported the creation of Yellowstone National Park; in 1884, on the retirement of Sherman, Sheridan became commanding general; in June 1888 he was awarded his fourth star; General Sheridan died shortly thereafter at Nonquitt, Massachusetts. He remains among the most influential soldiers in the nation's history.

2
THE UNION OFFENSIVE

On January 13, 1862, after two weeks of frenzied prepara-
tions, Curtis set his army in motion toward Springfield. During
the next month the Army of the Southwest struggled across the
Ozark Plateau. Progress was abysmally slow at first.
Inexperience and inclement weather sometimes brought the
long blue column to a complete stop. Heavy snowstorms were
followed by springlike thaws. A disgusted Union soldier
described the resulting situation as "mud without mercy." After
only a few days on the march it was clear to everyone why
armies avoided winter campaigns. Nevertheless, Curtis and his
troops persevered. As the weeks passed the pace quickened
and the Federals steadily closed in on Springfield.

Price was entirely unprepared for the unexpected appearance of a Union army in southwestern Missouri in the middle
of winter. He had neglected to fortify Springfield and he rightly
feared that the approaching army outnumbered his own.

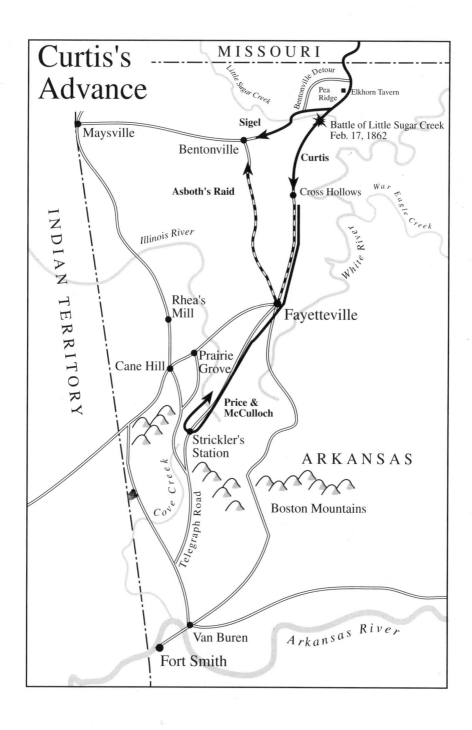

Curtis's Advance

MISSOURI

Little Sugar Creek

Bentonville Detour

Pea Ridge   ■ Elkhorn Tavern

Maysville

Sigel

Bentonville

★ Battle of Little Sugar Creek
Feb. 17, 1862

Curtis

Asboth's Raid

Cross Hollows

War Eagle Creek

INDIAN TERRITORY

Illinois River

White River

Rhea's Mill

Fayetteville

Prairie Grove

Cane Hill

Price & McCulloch

Strickler's Station

ARKANSAS

Cove Creek

Telegraph Road

Boston Mountains

Van Buren

Arkansas River

Fort Smith

Realizing his predicament, he once again called upon McCulloch for assistance, but due to McCulloch's absence in Virginia and a general breakdown in communications, no help was forthcoming from the Confederate forces in Arkansas. As the Union army came within sight, Price abruptly decided not to fight but to flee. He abandoned Springfield on February 12 and retreated to the south. If McCulloch would not join him in Missouri, he would join McCulloch in Arkansas.

Much to Price's surprise, Curtis followed. Unlike many other generals at this early stage of the war, Curtis understood that his primary objective was the neutralization of the opposing army, not the occupation of territory. After taking permanent possession of Springfield, he hurried after Price, determined to bring him to battle at the first opportunity. The result was the only true pursuit of one army by another in the Civil War.

For four days the two columns tramped along Telegraph (or Wire) Road, the primary route linking southwestern Missouri and northwestern Arkanas. Sharp engagements frequently took place between the Confederate rear guard and the Union vanguard. The weather turned intensely cold and soldiers in both armies endured snow, sleet, and freezing rain. "I felt like I was dying, I was so chilled," recalled Samuel McDaniel of the Missouri State Guard. "The snow was all over us, and our clothes frozen on our bodies." As the grinding pursuit went on, the trail of Price's army was marked by "crippled and demolished wagons, pots, pans, skillets, camp trumpery, dead and dying horses and mules, together with all manner of goods and chattels." Hundreds of exhausted Rebels gave up or were left behind. Curtis reported to Halleck that "more straggling prisoners are being taken than I know what to do with."

The hard-pressed Rebel column hurried across the state line into Arkansas on February 16. The next day the Army of the Southwest followed. In so doing Curtis not only entered Arkansas, he also invaded the Confederacy. While Union bands played patriotic and popular tunes including, appropriately enough, "The Arkansas Traveler," Curtis congratulated his cheering men for being the first Federal soldiers to set foot on the "virgin soil" of Arkansas. "Such yelling and whooping, it was glorious," Major John C. Black of the 37th Illinois informed his mother. Exhilarated by the unexpected success of his campaign thus far, Curtis sent a triumphant message to Halleck in St. Louis: "The flag of our Union again floats in Arkansas."

Apparently forgotten in all the excitement was the fact that the purpose of the Union operation was to enable Halleck to invade the Confederacy elsewhere. Neither Halleck nor Curtis had anticipated that a limited campaign designed to counter Price would take the Union army out of Missouri and into Arkansas. Curtis's southward surge into Rebeldom had taken on a life of its own.

Later that day, a few miles south of the Arkansas-Missouri state line, Curtis and his men marched past a rural hostelry called Elkhorn Tavern located on a broad tableland known to local settlers as Pea Ridge. A short distance ahead, on the south side of Little Sugar Creek, the vanguard of the Union column encountered a strong line of Confederate infantry and cavalry supported by artillery. After an initial engagement between mounted forces, the two sides blasted away at each other with artillery until sunset. Little Sugar Creek was the first taste of combat for most of Curtis's men. Captain Henry J. Cummings of the 4th Iowa probably expressed the sentiments of many Union soldiers when he informed his wife that "the roar of the cannon was loud and frequent and was very exciting."

In the gathering darkness Price withdrew down Telegraph Road to Cross Hollows, a dozen miles to the south. The clash at Little Sugar Creek on February 17 marked the first time that some of McCulloch's troops had fought alongside Price's men since Wilson's Creek six months earlier. An Arkansas soldier described the fight as "a right brisk skirmish," but it was more than that and casualties were correspondingly high. Thirteen Federals were killed and about twenty wounded. The Confederates lost up to twenty-six men killed.

Curtis camped for two days in the picturesque valley of Little Sugar Creek to allow his army to rest and recuperate. He studied the local terrain and took careful note of a line of towering bluffs that run along the north side of the valley. The bluffs form the abrupt southern edge of Pea Ridge and struck

Alexander S. Asboth: born Hungary 1811; Asboth was graduated from the Selmecbanya Academy and worked as a government engineer throughout Hungary; during the Hungarian independence movements of 1848, he followed the revolutionary Lojos Kossuth; Asboth then joined the deposed Kossuth in exile, first to Turkey and eventually to the United States in 1851; he became a U.S. citizen, settling in Missouri, and, at the outbreak of the Civil War, offered his services to the Union; General John C. Frémont personally appointed Asboth brigadier general of volunteers and chief of staff; although the government did not recognize the

appointment, Asboth served Frémont as assigned; he commanded a division and was wounded in the March 1862 Battle of Pea Ridge; officially appointed brigadier general, U.S. Volunteers, only days after the battle, he returned to division command and in 1863 assumed direction of the District of Columbus, Kentucky; transferred in August 1863, he commanded the District of West Florida; in October 1864 he was severely wounded in the face and arm during the Battle of Marianna, Florida; although the bullet remained lodged in his left cheek bone, Asboth returned to duty and served for the remainder of the war; brevetted major general, U.S.V., for war service he was mustered out in August 1865; in 1866 he was appointed U.S. minister to Argentina and Uruguay; he travelled to Paris to have the bullet removed from his cheek, but the wound never healed. General Asboth died at Buenos Aires in January 1868.

Curtis as an excellent defensive position. Curtis had an exaggerated notion of the strength of the Confederate position at Cross Hollows, which actually was a large cantonment rather than a fortified strongpoint. He therefore decided not to advance directly upon Cross Hollows but to swing around to the west by way of Bentonville so as to compel Price and McCulloch to retreat or be surrounded. On February 18 Curtis sent Brigadier General Alexander S. Asboth and a cavalry brigade on a reconnaissance in force to Bentonville. When Asboth reported that the rolling terrain west of Cross Hollows was clear of enemy soldiers, Curtis prepared to move his command in that direction.

Curtis did not know that the Confederates already were abandoning Cross Hollows. McCulloch had just returned from Virginia and reached Cross Hollows only a few hours after the fight at Little Sugar Creek. He received a tumultuous welcome from his troops, who cheered wildly and tossed their hats in the air at the sight of their long-absent commander. McCulloch was moved to tears by the experience. As he passed each regiment the laconic Texan removed his hat and said simply: "Men, I am glad to see you!" The response was deafening.

When he finally retired to his headquarters, McCulloch was shocked to learn of Price's headlong flight from Springfield and the presence of a Union army on Arkansas soil. McCulloch had laid out the cantonment at Cross Hollows and he knew better than anyone that the position was untenable. It was obvious to him that the combined armies would have to fall back even deeper into Arkansas. Price seemed to have regained his nerve despite the harrowing experience of the past few days. He inexplicably wanted to make a stand at Cross Hollows despite the unfavorable ground, but most of his subordinates sided with McCulloch.

The retreat resumed on February 19. The Confederates burned the complex of barracks, mills, and storehouses in Cross Hollows and trudged south in miserably cold weather.

The next day they reached Fayetteville, the principal town in northwestern Arkansas. Fayetteville was a major Confederate supply depot but McCulloch was unable to remove the tons of military stores because of a lack of transportation—most of his horses and mules were still in the Arkansas River valley. McCulloch decided to make everything available to the passing troops. A soldier in the 2d Missouri named I.V. Smith noted that "nearly every man in the regiment got a ham or a shoulder or a side of bacon, ran his bayonet through them and carried it in to camp." He added that "it was a novel sight to see so much meat on the march." Unfortunately, the disorganized method of distribution quickly degenerated into looting and vandalism as homes and businesses were ransacked.

The situation grew even worse the next day when McCulloch ordered all remaining supplies destroyed. Soldiers burned public buildings and warehouses filled with combustibles and defective ammunition. The resulting explosions spread the fires and destroyed several city blocks in the middle of town. Fayetteville thus gained the distinction of being perhaps the first Southern town—but hardly the last—to feel the hard hand of war. A disgusted Confederate surgeon called the sacking of Fayetteville "one of the most disgraceful scenes that I ever saw."

Burdened with food, clothing, jewelry, furniture, and even baby rattles, the Confederates staggered south another seventeen miles on Telegraph Road. They finally halted in the Boston Mountains, the extremely rugged southern escarpment of the Ozark Plateau. McCulloch's army camped along the Illinois River near Strickler's Station; Price's army bivouacked just to the west along Cove Creek. The long retreat that had begun ten days earlier at Springfield finally was over.

Word soon reached Curtis that the Confederates had abandoned Cross Hollows and fallen back into the Boston Mountains. Instead of pursuing, he paused to consider the strategic situation. Curtis now faced the two largest

Confederate armies west of the Mississippi, armies which had joined forces and overwhelmed Lyon at Wilson's Creek six months earlier. Curtis correctly concluded that the Rebels outnumbered his own small command by a substantial margin. Indeed, he was acutely aware that the Army of the Southwest was not only small, it was getting smaller. Attrition caused by hard marching and the need to garrison Springfield and other vital points along the line of communication had cost the Union army about one-fifth of its original manpower. Curtis had only about 10,000 men under his immediate command in Arkansas. Moreover, he now was over two hundred miles south of the railhead at Rolla and, despite Sheridan's best efforts, his supply situation was critical. Surgeon George Gordon of the 18th Indiana ominously noted that "it looks like starving if we do not save rations."

Curtis ultimately decided that he could best carry out his mission of securing Missouri by holding his position in northwestern Arkansas. He dispatched cavalry raids in various directions to gather information and keep the Confederates off balance. The largest of these operations, another reconnaissance in force led by Asboth, occupied what was left of Fayetteville on February 22-26. Despite the presence of a sizable number of Unionist citizens who hailed Asboth as a deliverer, Curtis reluctantly concluded that he could not hold Fayetteville because it was too far south, and far too close to the Rebel armies lurking just beyond in the Boston Mountains.

To facilitate foraging, Curtis took a calculated risk and divided his forces. He stationed two of his four divisions at Cross Hollows under his personal command, and placed the other two near Bentonville under the command of Brigadier General Franz Sigel, a German-born officer who would prove to be dangerously erratic. Curtis scattered smaller outposts across the countryside to monitor enemy activities. If the Confederates came storming out of the Boston Mountains, Curtis planned for the Army of the Southwest to unite and

Franz Sigel: born Grand Duchy of Baden (Germany) 1824; he was graduated from the military academy at Karlsrule in 1843 and served as a lieutenant in the service of Grand Duke Leopold; his participation in the failed Revolution of 1848 caused him to flee Germany; after stays in Switzerland and England, Sigel made his way to the United States in 1952; settling in New York, he taught school and held a commission in the New York Militia; removing to St. Louis, Missouri, he became director of schools and a leader in the large German community there; at the outbreak of the Civil War he offered his services to the Union and was appointed colonel of the 3d Missouri Infantry and, shortly thereafter, brigadier general of volunteers; he

participated in the capture of Camp Jackson and at Wilson's Creek in 1861; he commanded a division and played a conspicuous role in the Battle of Pea Ridge in March 1862; promoted to major general, Sigel transferred to the Eastern Theater, where he led a division in the Shenandoah Valley; he commanded the First Corps, Army of Virginia, during the Second Bull Run Campaign of 1862; thereafter, he directed the Eleventh Corps, Army of the Potomac, from September 1862 through February 1863, but saw little action and was forced to relinquish corps command due to poor health; returning to duty in March 1864, he assumed command of the Department of West Virginia; in May Sigel's command was routed at New Market, Virginia, by General John C. Breckinridge's Confederate force that included a contingent of cadets from the Virginia Military Institute; relieved of departmental command, Sigel took charge of the Reserve Division, Department of West Virginia, but saw little action for the rest of the war; he resigned his commission in May 1865; after the war he became active in Democratic politics and ran for numerous offices, eventually becoming a U.S. pension agent in New York by appointment of President Grover Cleveland; he died at New York City in 1902. Although his New Market defeat destroyed his military reputation, General Sigel deserved much credit for rallying thousands of German immigrants to the Union cause; "I fights mit Sigel" became a proud exclamation of German-born soldiers throughout the Federal army.

make a defensive stand atop the bluffs along the north side of Little Sugar Creek. The bluffs, he told his brother in Ohio, were the place "where I knew I could make the best fight."

Despite his isolated position and his precarious logistical situation, Curtis was determined to stand firm in Arkansas and prevent Price from returning to Missouri. He telegraphed Halleck: "Shall be on the alert, holding as securely as possible." What happened next would be up to the Confederates.

3
THE CONFEDERATE COUNTEROFFENSIVE

Van Dorn was at his headquarters in Pocahontas when he learned of the loss of Springfield and the disastrous series of events that followed. He immediately set out on an exhausting nine-day journey across central Arkansas to take personal command of the two Confederate armies in the Boston Mountains. Somewhere along the way he fell into an icy stream, became ill, and had to complete the trip in an ambulance. He finally reached Strickler's Station on March 3 and assumed command. Van Dorn demoted McCulloch and Price to division commanders, a step that both men expected and accepted. The new commander made no other significant changes except to give the combined force a name: the Army of the West.

During a conference with his new subordinates on the day

of his arrival, Van Dorn learned that Curtis had dispersed his army into two widely separated camps. This information galvanized Van Dorn and he impulsively decided to launch a full-scale counteroffensive the next morning. The three Confederate generals quickly decided on a course of action. The Army of the West would leave the Boston Mountains and march north to Bentonville. There the Confederates would turn west and overwhelm the two Union divisions under Sigel. Then the Confederates would turn east and do the same to the remaining two Union divisions under Curtis at Cross Hollows. This was a classic military gambit known as "defeating the enemy in detail." With Curtis's force out of the way, the way to Missouri would be open. Van Dorn and the victorious Army of the West would press on towards St. Louis "then Huzzah!"

The key to success was the road junction at Bentonville. If Van Dorn reached that point before Curtis realized what was happening, the Confederate army would be between the two much smaller Union forces. Speed was required to achieve the essential element of surprise, so Van Dorn stipulated that each Confederate soldier carry only his weapon, forty rounds of ammunition, a blanket, and three day's rations. An ammunition train would follow the troops. All else was to be left behind in the Boston Mountains.

The central flaw in all of this was Van Dorn's assumption that the operation would go exactly as planned. After the inevitable victory he expected his men and animals to subsist on captured Yankee rations and forage. He apparently gave no thought to alternate sources of supply or to the possibility that things might go awry. Van Dorn's overconfidence was matched by his impulsiveness. He did not allow himself time to get to know his principal subordinates, to familiarize himself with the geography of the region, to reorganize the two very different armies awkwardly joined together under his command, or even to recover from his illness. A few days might have made all the difference.

Determined to use all available manpower, Van Dorn ordered Brigadier General Albert Pike in the nearby Indian Territory to mobilize Confederate Indian troops and rendezvous with the Army of the West at Bentonville. Pike was properly reluctant to do so because the treaties he had negotiated between the Confederacy and the Five Civilized Tribes— the Cherokees, Choctaws, Creeks, Chickasaws, and Seminoles—stipulated that Indian soldiers were not to be used outside the Indian Territory without their approval. Nevertheless, when Pike raised the issue he learned that some

Albert Pike: born Massachusetts 1809; when plans to attend Harvard fell through, he moved to Arkansas; edited a newspaper in Little Rock and practiced law; as a

lawyer, he pursued Indian grievances in Federal courts; served in the Mexican War; a highly-regarded author and poet, Pike became a prominent land owner in Arkansas; at the outbreak of the Civil War he was sent by the Confederate government to negotiate alliances with the Cherokee, Chickasaw, Choctaw, Creek, and Seminole Nations; brigadier general August 1861; headed the Department of Indian Territory; led Indian troops in the Battle of Elkhorn Tavern, Arkansas, in March 1862, but drew blame for his command's poor conduct during the battle; subsequent differences with General Thomas C. Hindman, commander of the Trans-Mississippi Department, and accusations of atrocities committed by Pike's Indian troops resulted in Pike's resignation in July 1862; following accusations of insanity and disloyalty leveled by General Douglas Cooper, Pike's resignation was accepted in November; he passed the remainder of the war in Arkansas and Texas, but, as a distrusted figure, he saw no further duty; after the war he moved to Washington, D.C., where he resumed his writing; a devoted Freemason, he wrote *The Morals and Dogma of the Ancient and Accepted Scottish Rite* (1872); an earlier work, *Prose and Poems Written in the Western Country* (1834) was widely praised. General Pike died at Washington in 1891.

Indians were willing to participate in the operation if paid in advance. Despite deep misgivings, Pike mobilized two small Cherokee regiments. One of the regimental commanders was Colonel Stand Watie, the only Indian to earn general's stars on either side in the Civil War.

The Confederate counteroffensive to liberate Missouri began on March 4 when Van Dorn led his command out of the

Stand Watie: born Cherokee Nation (Georgia) 1806; attended mission school; became a planter and published a Cherokee newspaper; a leading member of the faction that supported Cherokee resettlement in the West; signed the Treaty of Echota in 1835 that led to the Cherokee removal to Indian Territory (Oklahoma) and bitterly divided the Cherokee Nation—the other leaders of the pro-removal faction were all killed; relocated to Indian Territory; a slaveowner, he organized the Knights of the Golden Circle; at the outset of the Civil War the division among Cherokees left Watie the leader of a minority favoring the Confederacy; he raised a regiment of Cherokees for Confederate service and in July 1861 became colonel of the Cherokee Mounted Rifles; fought at Wilson's Creek, Missouri, in August and further helped secure the Confederacy's hold on the Indian Territory in the Battle of Chustenahlah; led his Indian troops in the Battle of Elkhorn Tavern, Arkansas, in March 1862; elected principal chief of the Confederate Cherokees in August; over the next three years Watie's command engaged in numerous raids, small actions, and skirmishes in the Indian Territory and surrounding areas; commissioned brigadier general in May 1864 and given command of an Indian brigade; finally surrendered in June 1865—the last Confederate general to do so; after the war he engaged in planting and pursued business interests in the Indian Territory; he died at his home in 1871. Recognized for his personal bravery and loyalty to the Confederacy, General Watie was the only Indian to become a general officer during the war. His Indian troops proved to be capable raiders and fought effectively in spontaneous actions; they were, however, poorly suited for pitched battle.

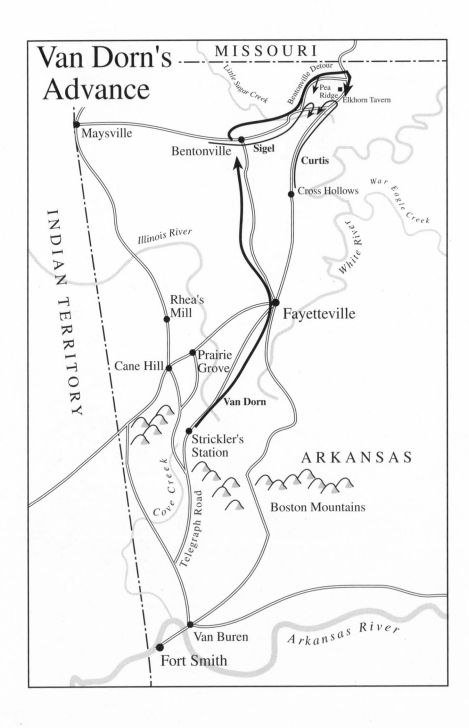

Van Dorn's Advance

MISSOURI

Little Sugar Creek

Bentonville Detour

Pea Ridge

Elkhorn Tavern

Maysville

Bentonville

Sigel

Curtis

Cross Hollows

War Eagle Creek

White River

Illinois River

I N D I A N   T E R R I T O R Y

Rhea's Mill

Fayetteville

Prairie Grove

Cane Hill

Van Dorn

Strickler's Station

A R K A N S A S

Cove Creek

Boston Mountains

Telegraph Road

Van Buren

Arkansas River

Fort Smith

Boston Mountains. The 16,000 men and 65 cannon of the Army of the West comprised the largest and best-equipped Confederate military force ever assembled west of the Mississippi River. The Confederates had a three-to-two advantage in manpower and a four-to-three advantage in artillery. It was a historic moment: no Confederate army in the Civil War ever marched off to battle with greater numerical superiority.

Unfortunately for the cause of Southern independence, the march to Bentonville—and ultimately to Pea Ridge—was a disaster. Van Dorn was feverish and distracted. Bouncing along Telegraph Road in an enclosed ambulance at the head of the column, he set an unrealistically rapid pace. McCulloch's troops had been in winter quarters for months and were unprepared for such a strenuous effort. Soon the roadside was littered with hundreds of winded soldiers hobbled by blistered feet. Even Price's Missourians, initially overjoyed at the thought of returning home, became disgruntled and remarked sarcastically that Van Dorn "had forgotten he was riding and we were walking." That same day a late winter blizzard swept across the Ozark Plateau, dropping temperatures and covering the road with ice and snow. Progress slowed to a crawl and the column finally halted for the night amidst the charred ruins of Fayetteville.

The next day, March 5, the Confederates plodded north across a wintry landscape and camped at Elm Springs, about halfway between Fayetteville and Bentonville. "I will never forget that night," wrote a Missouri soldier. "It had turned bitter cold....We had no tents and only one blanket to each man. We built log heaps and set them afire to warm the ground to have a place on which to lie, and I remember well the next day there were several holes burned in my uniform by sparks left on the ground." The following morning the Confederates ate the last of their rations and set out for Bentonville, twelve miles to the north. Despite the slow pace and the deteriorating condition of his men and animals, Van Dorn remained confident that his plan to take Curtis by surprise was working.

Unknown to Van Dorn, a Unionist resident of Fayetteville and a spy planted in the Rebel ranks both reached Curtis at Cross Hollows on March 5 and informed him of the Confederate advance. It was fortunate for the Union cause that they did so, for up to that point the terrible weather had prevented Federal patrols from detecting the massive enemy column moving north toward Bentonville. Curtis did not hesitate. He assumed the startling information was correct—"They are coming sure," he informed Sigel—and ordered an immediate concentration of his forces at Little Sugar Creek as planned. "It was now our turn to run," observed Corporal Sam Black of the 1st Iowa Battery. The Federals struck their tents and hurried through the darkness toward the rendezvous point, struggling against the same miserable wintry conditions as the Confederates. "It was snowing and most intensely cold," wrote Captain Cummings to his wife in Iowa. "I never suffered so much in my life." Deserted buildings along the roads were set afire to light the way.

By the morning of March 6, nearly all of the Army of the Southwest was in place on the north side of Little Sugar Creek. Curtis was an experienced engineer and he personally laid out a line of earthworks atop the bluffs. All that day Union soldiers prepared rifle pits and redoubts, cleared fields of fire, and awaited the arrival of the enemy.

The only Federals who failed to reach Little Sugar Creek without incident were six hundred men who served as rear guard for Sigel's two divisions. This detachment was personally commanded by Sigel, who unaccountably tarried behind to eat a hearty breakfast in a Bentonville hotel. Sigel and his little command were nearly cut off by the vanguard of the approaching Confederate army, a large cavalry force led by Brigadier General James M. McIntosh. After a four-mile running fight across snow-covered fields and roads east of Bentonville, Sigel finally shook off his pursuers and joined Curtis at Little Sugar Creek.

When Van Dorn reached Bentonville a short time later he

realized that his plan to defeat the Union army in detail had failed. The Army of the Southwest was reunited in an impregnable blufftop location along Little Sugar Creek, while the Confederate army was in desperate straits. After three extremely difficult days, men and animals were hungry and exhausted. Straggling had become epidemic. "Such a worn-out set of men I never saw," remembered Sergeant William Kinney of the 3rd Louisiana. "They had not one single mouthfull of food to eat." Van Dorn refused to consider falling back to the Boston Mountains despite the desperate state of affairs. He was determined to strike the Yankees a blow, seize their supplies, and push into Missouri. As darkness fell on a singularly dismal Confederate encampment, Pike straggled in from the Indian Territory with about eight hundred mounted Cherokees—all he could convince to accompany him. He brought no additional food or forage.

That evening Van Dorn conferred with his generals. McCulloch told Van Dorn of a lane that led around Curtis's right flank and intersected Telegraph Road near the Arkansas-Missouri state line, deep in the Federal rear. If the Confederates could reach Telegraph Road in force, Curtis would be cut off and might be compelled to surrender. Van Dorn impulsively decided to march immediately. For the first time in months McCulloch and Price agreed on something: both men were aghast at the thought of a night march with the men and animals in such pitiful condition. McCulloch appealed to Van Dorn "for God sake to let the poor, worn-out and hungry soldiers rest and sleep that night...and then attack the next morning." But Van Dorn was adamant; he insisted that the army move at once. Apparently undeterred by the misgivings of his generals and indifferent to the deteriorating condition of his command, Van Dorn set his maneuver in motion a few hours before midnight on March 6.

The march on the Bentonville Detour, as the roundabout lane was known, was a terrible experience for the Army of the

West. It had finally stopped snowing but now the temperature began to plunge. The shivering column shuffled along at a snail's pace, delayed for hours by frigid streams and tangled barricades of trees felled by the Federals to obstruct precisely such a flanking maneuver. Van Dorn's numerical superiority continued to erode as hundreds of men collapsed by the roadside, some of whom would perish from exposure. At dawn on March 7, Price's Division reached Telegraph Road, but Pike's tiny Indian brigade at the tail of the attenuated column was still back at Little Sugar Creek.

Van Dorn now made another ill-considered decision. To save time, Van Dorn and Price's Division would proceed south on Telegraph Road on the east side of a rocky hill called Big Mountain. McCulloch's Division and Pike's Brigade, several miles back along the Bentonville Detour, would turn south on Ford Road on the west side of Big Mountain. The two halves of the Army of the West would reunite around midday at Elkhorn Tavern atop the broad expanse of Pea Ridge. There the Confederates would deploy for battle and advance upon the unsuspecting Federals from the north. Van Dorn had no qualms about dividing his army in the presence of the enemy because he believed the Union army was still in its fortifications at Little Sugar Creek, expecting an attack from the south.

4
THE BATTLE OF PEA RIDGE: LEETOWN

Union patrols detected the Confederate movement on the Bentonville Detour before dawn on March 7. Curtis was surprised at the report. He expected the impulsive Van Dorn to launch an all-out assault against the Little Sugar Creek fortifications and incorrectly assumed that the presence of Confederate forces so far to the north was a diversion. Nevertheless, Curtis could not permit enemy soldiers to rampage around in his rear. He launched two spoiling attacks intended to intercept and delay the approaching enemy columns on either side of Big Mountain.

Shortly before noon on March 7 Colonel Peter J. Osterhaus withdrew his division from the Little Sugar Creek fortifications and headed toward McCulloch's column moving around the west side of Big Mountain on Ford Road. Osterhaus rode ahead of his division in order to familiarize himself with the rolling countryside atop Pea Ridge. He was accompanied only by a small force of cavalry and three cannon. A mile or so north of the hamlet of Leetown the Union advance party

Peter J. Osterhaus: born Prussia 1823; Osterhaus received a military education in his native Prussia but, like so many others of his generation, he was forced to leave Europe after participation in the revolutions of 1848; he settled in the United States in the early 1850s, first in Illinois and then in St. Louis, where he found a home among that city's large German population; at the outbreak of the Civil War he served the Union as major of a Missouri battalion, with which he participated in the capture of Camp Jackson and in the Battle of Wilson's Creek; commissioned

colonel of the 12th Missouri Infantry, he commanded a division in the Battle of Pea Ridge in March 1862; promoted that August to brigadier general, he held numerous commands in the Trans-Mississippi; in January 1863 he moved east of the Mississippi to participate in the Vicksburg Campaign; he commanded a division in the Army of the Tennessee and was wounded in the fighting at Big Black River Bridge; continuing with the Army of Tennessee, he performed admirably during the Chattanooga Campaign; during the Atlanta Campaign of 1864, Osterhaus was frequently absent from his command but nonetheless garnered a promotion to major general of volunteers; he periodically directed the Fifteenth Corps in General William T. Sherman's March to the Sea but, in January 1865, was transferred to the Military Division of West Mississippi and served as chief of staff to General E.R.S. Canby during the Mobile Campaign; mustered out of volunteer service in January 1866, he was U.S. consul at Lyons, France, from 1866 to 1877, while maintaining a residence and business in St.Louis; he later served as deputy consul at Mannheim, Germany, from 1898-1900; placed on the army's retired list as a brigadier general by act of Congress in 1905, General Osterhaus died at Duisburg, Germany, in 1917, only weeks before the U.S. declared war on the general's homeland.

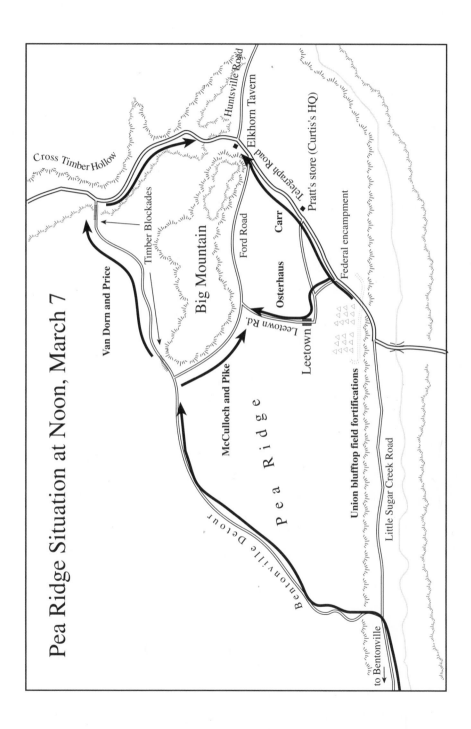

Pea Ridge Situation at Noon, March 7

emerged from a belt of trees onto Wiley Foster's farm and came to an abrupt halt. There Osterhaus saw, not the modest-sized diversionary force he had expected to encounter, but McCulloch's entire division plodding eastward toward Elkhorn Tavern on Ford Road. Osterhaus was shocked by the sight of so many thousands of Rebels—it seemed as though he had stumbled upon half of the Confederate army! "Notwithstanding my command was entirely inadequate to the overwhelming masses opposed to me," he reported without exaggeration, "I could not hesitate in my course of action." Osterhaus unlimbered his three cannon and opened fire against the tightly packed formation of Confederate infantry, cavalry, and artillery. These opening shots of the battle of Pea Ridge struck down dozens of Arkansas and Texas cavalrymen.

Now it was McCulloch's turn to be surprised. Like all the Confederate generals, he believed the Federals were still in their fortifications at Little Sugar Creek facing south. He was looking forward, both literally and figuratively, to meeting Van Dorn and Price at Elkhorn Tavern, which was only two miles ahead on Ford Road. The last thing he expected was an attack from his right rear. After a few minutes of total confusion in the Confederate ranks, McCulloch sent McIntosh and his 3,000 cavalrymen sweeping across a wheatfield toward the Federal position. Six regiments of Arkansas and Texas horsemen overwhelmed Osterhaus's small command. "In every direction I could see my comrades falling," recalled Henry Dysart of the 3d Iowa Cavalry. "Horses frencied and riderless, ran to and fro. Men and horses ran in collision crushing each other to the ground. Dismounted troopers ran in every direction. Officers tried to rally their men but order gave way to confusion. The scene baffles description." The Confederates easily routed the Federals and captured their three cannon.

A few hundred yards to the west, Pike conformed to McIntosh's movements by ordering his command to attack as well. The Cherokees, some mounted, others on foot, picked their way through a patch of woods and drove off two isolated companies of Union cavalry. (A well-known Currier and Ives print is largely responsible for the persistent myth that the Cherokees took part in the massed cavalry charge, and that they were dressed in warbonnets and other inappropriate Plains Indian regalia. The facts are that the Indians fought on their own in the woods and wore the same unmilitary mix of store-bought and homespun clothing as did practically every other Southerner in the Army of the West. Their modest contribution to the Confederate cause at Pea Ridge was tarnished when a handful of Cherokees murdered and scalped several

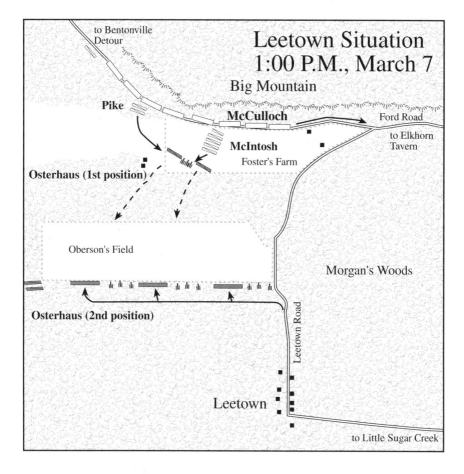

Leetown Situation
1:00 P.M., March 7

Federal soldiers in the woods.)

Osterhaus and the surviving members of his advance party fell back through the belt of trees and across a large cornfield owned by Samuel Oberson. On the south side of the field he met the rest of his division and formed a line of battle facing north. Osterhaus was outnumbered better than four to one. He had only three regiments of Illinois, Missouri, and Indiana infantry—fewer than 1,600 men—and three batteries of artillery. McCulloch's powerful force had been weakened by straggling but still consisted of about 7,000 men and four batteries of artillery, more than enough to sweep aside Osterhaus's command if properly handled.

Rattled but determined to hold his ground as long as possible, Osterhaus sent a message to Curtis stating that he had met the enemy and urgently needed reinforcements. He then readied his command for another Rebel onslaught. Though the Confederates were out of sight on the north side of the belt of trees, Osterhaus ordered his artillery to fire over the trees in hopes of causing some disorder in the enemy ranks. This act had unforeseen results.

The first salvo of Union shells landed among the Cherokees. The Indians had never experienced artillery fire before and were terrified by the explosions that seemed to come out of nowhere. They fled from the field and played only a marginal role in the remainder of the battle. The intensity of the barrage also convinced McCulloch that he could not push on to Elkhorn Tavern and leave such a substantial enemy force in his rear. He made the critical decision to deploy his entire division at Leetown. Amidst all the noise and confusion during and after the unexpected clash on Foster's farm, the exhausted McCulloch neglected to inform Van Dorn that the reunion of the two halves of the Army of the West at Elkhorn Tavern would be delayed. Osterhaus had suffered a tactical reverse at the outset of the battle, but his tenacious tactics had achieved his primary mission of disrupting Confederate plans.

McCulloch was confident of success as he prepared for a general assault against Osterhaus's thin blue line on the south side of Oberson's Field. "In one hour they will be ours," he remarked to an aide. He rode along the forming Confederate line of battle, conferring with subordinates and encouraging his weary Arkansas and Texas soldiers. At the extreme right or western end of the line he decided to turn south and push through a gap in the belt of trees to observe the Federals for himself. "I will ride forward a little and reconnoiter the enemy's position. You boys remain here," he told his staff, "your gray horses will attract the fire of the sharpshooters."

McCulloch had developed the habit of personal reconnaissance during his long career in the Texas Rangers. The technique had served him well in the past, but at Pea Ridge it proved fatal. Osterhaus had posted two companies of the 36th Illinois as skirmishers behind a rail fence running along the north edge of Oberson's Field. The skirmishers saw McCulloch ride directly toward them. Clad in a black suit and mounted on a tall horse, the general was sharply outlined against a wintry blue sky when he passed over a small rise. Dozens of Union soldiers steadied their rifles on the fence and fired a volley. McCulloch tumbled from the saddle, killed by a bullet through the heart. Because of the heavy foliage, no one in the Rebel ranks saw him fall.

For nearly an hour the entire Confederate force at Leetown remained immobile, awaiting orders to advance from McCulloch, who seemed to have vanished into thin air. The general's fate remained unknown until an Arkansas regiment advanced to drive off the Federal skirmishers and literally stumbled across his body. Command of the division finally passed to McIntosh, who immediately ordered the general assault that McCulloch had prepared. Before the order could be passed along the line, however, McIntosh foolishly advanced through the belt of trees alongside his old regiment, the 2d Arkansas Mounted Rifles. As he emerged from the woods he was struck down like his predecessor by a bullet through the heart, a victim of a volley from another company of the 36th Illinois. With McIntosh's death the abortive Confederate assault abruptly sputtered out west of Leetown Road. The few regiments that had advanced, or were preparing to advance, wavered and then fell back to Foster's farm without ever engaging the outnumbered Union force in Oberson's Field.

Jefferson C. Davis: born Indiana 1828; Davis fought in the Mexican War as a teen-aged volunteer; commissioned into the regular army as 2d lieutenant of artillery in 1848, gaining promotion to 1st lieutenant in 1852; he was on duty during the bombardment of Fort Sumter in April 1861; promoted to captain in May, Davis entered the volunteer army in August as colonel of the 22d Indiana Infantry, with which he fought at Wilson's Creek, Missouri; promoted to brigadier general, U.S. Volunteers, to rank from December, he led a division at Pea Ridge, Arkansas, in March 1862

and at Corinth, Mississippi; in September 1862 at Louisville, Kentucky, Davis initiated an altercation with his superior, General William "Bull" Nelson, in which Davis shot and killed Nelson, reportedly in cold blood; no charges were ever filed and Davis returned to duty, commanding a division in the Army of the Cumberland at Stone's River, Chickamauga, and during the Atlanta Campaign; in August 1864 he assumed command of the Fourteenth Corps, with the brevet rank of major general, U.S. Volunteers; he led the corps with distinction for the remainder of the Atlanta Campaign, in General William T. Sherman's March to the Sea, and in the Carolinas Campaign of 1865; brevetted through major general, U.S. Army, Davis never received promotion to the full rank of major general of volunteers, for which he was entitled and repeatedly recommended; although embittered by this perceived injustice, he continued in the regular army as colonel of the 23d Infantry, exercising departmental command in Alaska and participating in the campaign against the Modoc Indians in California; General Davis died at Chicago in 1879. Although his killing of General Nelson doubtless affected his promotion and likely prevented a more prominent role in the post-war army, Davis was a competent and often outstanding officer.

The sudden loss of both McCulloch and McIntosh paralyzed the right and center of the Confederate line west of Leetown Road. The left of the Confederate line was deployed east of the road in a densely forested area known as Morgan's Woods. This portion of the line was under the command of Colonel Louis Hébert, a capable Louisiana Acadian who was now the ranking officer in the division. Stationed deep in the woods, however, Hébert was unaware that McCulloch and McIntosh had been killed and that he was in overall command. When he heard the intermittent firing to the west that felled his superiors, he assumed it marked the beginning of the general assault. Hébert waited impatiently for the order to advance. Around 3 P.M. he finally decided to go forward on his own and led four Arkansas and Louisiana regiments south toward the exposed right flank of Osterhaus's line.

The delay occasioned by the death of the two generals had disastrous consequences for the Confederates. Union reinforcements arrived at Leetown just in time to block Hébert's assault. When Curtis received Osterhaus's message begging for support, he dispatched a division commanded by Colonel Jefferson C. Davis, a man with one of the most distinctive names in the Union Army. Davis pulled his troops out of the Little Sugar Creek fortifications and reached the Leetown area in mid-afternoon. As a Union band tootled "Dixie," Davis deployed his four small Illinois and Indiana regiments—about 1,400 men—in Morgan's Woods on Osterhaus's right and sent them forward.

Hébert's Confederates and Davis's Federals plowed blindly into each other and opened fire at extremely close range. "Suddenly something like a tremendous peal of thunder opened all along our front," recalled William Watson of the 3rd Louisiana. Staggered by the shock, both lines ground to a halt and an intense fight erupted in the tangled woods. An Illinois soldier recalled that the air around him was "literally filled with leaden hail. Balls would whiz by our ears, cut off bushes closely, and even cut our clothes." The Federals lay down to avoid the deadly fire, an unusual tactic so early in the war. Captain Henry Curtis, Jr., of the 37th Illinois told his mother that his men "would have been utterly annihilated" had he not "fought them flat on their bellies on the ground." On both sides formations dissolved and some units became little more than armed mobs stumbling around in the smoky thicket.

Hébert's men gradually pushed the Federals back. At one point in the struggle at least one hundred Confederates emerged from Morgan's Woods and surged across Leetown Road toward a Federal battery in the southeastern corner of

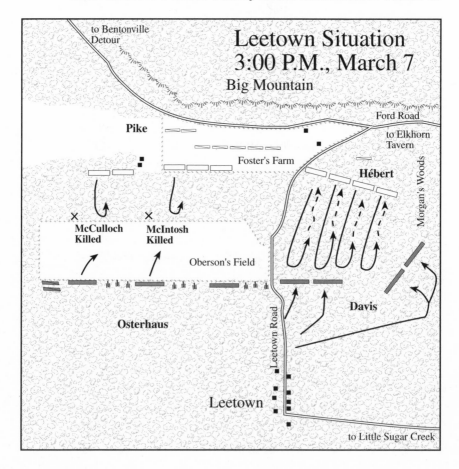

Oberson's Field. The oncoming Rebels were momentarily brought to a halt by Captain William P. Black of the 37th Illinois, who stood in front of the imperiled battery and blasted away with a Colt repeating rifle until being wounded. Black's heroism allowed the artillerymen to save four of their six cannons and earned him a Medal of Honor. For a moment it seemed as if Hébert had achieved a breakthrough, but Union regiments to left and right of the battery wheeled toward the Rebels and drove them back into the woods. As the afternoon wore on, more and more Confederates lost heart and drifted to the rear, weakened by hunger and the rigors of the three-day march. Hébert and two regimental commanders—Colonel William F. Tunnard of the 3rd Louisiana and Colonel William C. Mitchell of the 14th Arkansas—became disoriented with fatigue and drifted away from their own men. All three officers were captured, severely compounding the leadership problem that paralyzed McCulloch's Division.

When Hébert's attack stalled, Davis sent two Indiana regiments around the left flank of the disintegrating Confederate formation. The Union counterattack was hampered by poor visibility in the dense woods but it had the desired effect. "They were in a thick brushwood and we could not see them, only occasionally," stated E.E. Johnson of the 18th Indiana, "but we peppered them down as fast as we could see them." After a brief struggle the Confederate left flank crumbled and Hébert's force gave up the fight altogether. Survivors fled northward and poured out of Morgan's Woods onto Foster's Farm, where they discovered that over two-thirds of McCulloch's Division had been standing idle during the battle.

The failure of Hébert's unsupported attack, and the loss of Hébert himself, were the final blows to the ill-starred Confederate effort at Leetown. Now essentially leaderless, the officers and men of McCulloch's Division milled around waiting for someone to tell them what to do. Pike was the ranking officer and after some hesitation he attempted to assume command, but many officers refused to recognize his authority. Pike eventually led about half of McCulloch's Division away from Leetown toward Elkhorn Tavern on the Bentonville Detour. In so doing he inexplicably abandoned the other half of the division, which remained behind or drifted away from the battle toward Bentonville. Finally, Colonel Elkanah Greer of the 3rd Texas Cavalry took command of the scattered Confederate forces around Leetown and withdrew behind Big Mountain. By late afternoon on March 7 the struggle near Leetown was over.

The four hours of confused, sporadic fighting on Foster's Farm, Oberson's Field, and in Morgan's Woods had significant consequences. Outnumbered Union troops, blessed with good fortune and able commanders, had killed or captured three senior Confederate officers and wrecked a powerful Confederate force. But most important of all, the clash near Leetown kept the Army of the West divided.

5

THE BATTLE OF PEA RIDGE:
ELKHORN TAVERN

While McCulloch's Division unraveled during the afternoon of March 7 at Leetown, a much larger engagement raged two miles to the east in the vicinity of Elkhorn Tavern. Earlier that morning, as noted above, Curtis had launched two spoiling attacks. The first was commanded by Osterhaus, the second by

Colonel Eugene A. Carr, a steady regular army officer. Carr pulled half of his division out of the Little Sugar Creek fortifications and hurried up Telegraph Road along the east side of Big Mountain. He deployed his three Iowa and Illinois regiments and a battery—about 1,400 men—along the

Elkhorn tavern

northern escarpment of Pea Ridge near Elkhorn Tavern. The thin Union line was centered on Telegraph Road and looked down into Cross Timber Hollow, a deep and narrow valley. It was an immensely strong position and Carr was content to

Eugene A. Carr: born New York 1830; Carr was graduated from the U.S. Military Academy in 1850, nineteenth in his class of forty-four; commissioned 2d lieutenant and posted to the Mounted Rifles, he served on the frontier; promoted to 1st lieutenant, he was wounded in action against Indians near Fort Davis, Texas, in 1854; in 1858 he received a captaincy in the 1st Cavalry (redesignated the 4th Cavalry in 1861) and was serving in that capacity at the outbreak of the Civil War; he led his cavalry company in the Battle of Wilson's Creek, after which he entered

the volunteer service as colonel of the 3d Illinois Cavalry; Carr was conspicuous for his skill and bravery during the Battle of Pea Ridge, where he commanded both a cavalry brigade and an infantry division and was wounded three times, refusing to quit the field; for his exploits at Pea Ridge he was promoted to brigadier general, U.S. Volunteers, and later received the Congressional Medal of Honor; he commanded an infantry division in the Vicksburg Campaign but returned to Arkansas to command a cavalry division in the capture of Little Rock and in General Frederick Steele's Camden Expedition; from May through December 1864, Carr commanded the District of Little Rock; in the closing stages of the war, he commanded an infantry division in the Sixteenth Corps, Department of the Gulf, in General E.R.S. Canby's capture of Mobile; brevetted through major general in both regular and volunteer organizations, Carr mustered out of the volunteers in January 1866; continuing in the regular army, he reverted to his substantive rank of major, 5th Cavalry; he became one of the army's most prolific and talented Indian fighters, conducting numerous campaigns, most notably against the Apaches in Arizona; he was promoted to lieutenant colonel in 1873, colonel 1879, and brigadier general in 1892; he was retired in 1893 and died at Washington, D.C., in 1910. Despite his splendid Civil War service, General Carr is best remembered for his Indian War exploits.

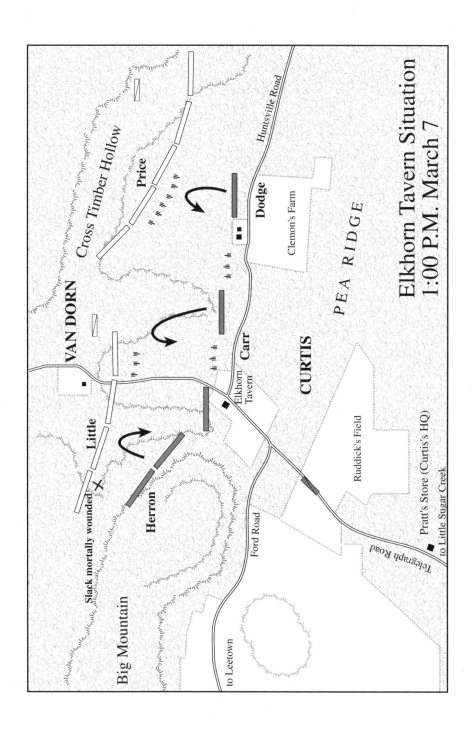

Elkhorn Tavern Situation
1:00 P.M. March 7

wait for the Confederates to come to him.

He did not have long to wait. Price's Division, personally led by Van Dorn, approached from the north on Telegraph Road. The division had been greatly reduced by straggling and numbered only about 5,000 men, but it included ten artillery batteries. Around noon the weary Confederates began to trudge up the steep slope that led from Cross Timber Hollow to the top of Pea Ridge. Fighting suddenly erupted as the leading Confederates clashed with a strong line of Federal skirmishers. Van Dorn, like McCulloch, was surprised to encounter Union troops so far north of Little Sugar Creek. He deployed Price's Division and sent it up the slope, expecting to brush aside whatever enemy contingent lay in his path.

Carr also was surprised as he watched the Confederate line of battle unfold in Cross Timber Hollow. Like Osterhaus, he had not expected to meet such a powerful enemy force. Nevertheless, like his valiant counterpart at Leetown, Carr decided to attack immediately despite the formidable odds. He sent an urgent plea for help to Curtis then got down to business. "Give them hell boys," he shouted above the rising din of battle. "Don't let them have it all their own way, give them hell." For the next two hours Carr repeatedly led his outnumbered infantry and artillery down the slope to break up the oncoming Confederate formation, then retired to his original position along the escarpment. It was a performance that earned him three wounds and a Medal of Honor.

Price's Missourians were exhausted, both physically and mentally, and they recoiled in the face of Carr's aggressive tactics. Van Dorn was puzzled at the unexpected course of events and assumed a defensive position near the bottom of Cross Timber Hollow. He probably expected McCulloch's Division to arrive at any moment along Ford Road and drive Carr away from Elkhorn Tavern. In the meantime he was content to skirmish and exchange artillery fire with the Yankees. Several hours would pass before Van Dorn learned that McCulloch's Division was fatally embroiled two miles to the west at Leetown. The decision to wait in Cross Timber Hollow was understandable, but it proved to be a critical error, for it gave Curtis time to reinforce Carr with the rest of his division. Two hours after the start of the engagement, Carr's thin ranks were bolstered by the arrival of another 1,000 men and a second battery from Little Sugar Creek.

Throughout the afternoon a furious exchange of artillery fire gradually filled Cross Timber Hollow with smoke. Confused skirmishing flared all along the steep rocky slope as soldiers of both sides blundered about in the thickening haze. "The smoke from the guns settled like a cloud upon the field," wrote an observer. "As the day advanced this cloud grew more and more dense, and long before nightfall the contending masses of infantry were unable to discern each other, except at very short range." During one sharp but murky clash, Confederate Colonel William Y. Slack went forward to see what was happening and was mortally wounded. A short time later Price was struck in the arm by a bullet. He stayed on the field but by the end of the day command of his Missouri division effectively passed to Colonel Henry Little.

A considerable amount of time passed before Van Dorn grasped the overall tactical situation, for he heard nothing from McCulloch and he could see almost nothing from his position at the bottom of Cross Timber Hollow. Around mid-afternoon he finally learned that McCulloch's Division was bogged down at Leetown, though he did not yet know that McCulloch was dead. About the same time he belatedly realized that Price's Division was much larger than Carr's force. Shaking off his lethargy, Van Dorn directed Price to extend his line beyond the flanks of the shorter Union line. Late in the afternoon Price's left finally reached the top of the escarpment a mile east of Elkhorn Tavern, well beyond Carr's right flank. Van Dorn ordered a general assault: the Confederate right would attack uphill and strike the Federals near the tavern, while the Confederate left would roll up the Federal right flank atop Pea Ridge.

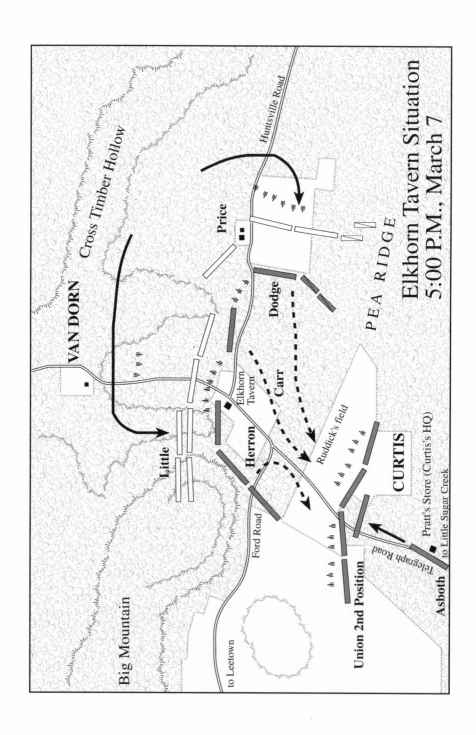

Elkhorn Tavern Situation
5:00 P.M., March 7

It took time to maneuver tired troops in such difficult terrain and the Confederates struck with barely an hour of daylight remaining. Fierce fighting erupted all along the slope on both sides of Telegraph Road. Nathan S. Harwood of the 9th Iowa, stationed near Elkhorn Tavern, heard and saw the Rebels come up the hill "with a yell and a fury that had a tendency to make each hair on one's head to stand on its particular end." Asa Payne of the 3d Missouri recalled vivid details of the assault from a different perspective. "The Federal line was in full view and I could hear something going zip, zip all around and could see the dust flying out of the trees and the limbs and twigs seemed to be in a commotion from the concussion of the guns." After a furious struggle Payne and his comrades overwhelmed the outnumbered Union forces and captured the tavern. Colonel Francis J. Herron led the 9th Iowa in a desperate rear guard defense that earned him a Medal of Honor, but he was wounded and captured.

A quarter-mile to the east, on a farm owned by Rufus Clemon, the Missourians had a tougher time, for a Union brigade commanded by Colonel Grenville M. Dodge fought from behind a breastwork of logs and easily repulsed several assaults. "I mowed them down in mounds," was how an exultant Dodge described the situation. "They charged us time and time again but they could not move us." Eventually, however, the Iowans were outflanked by superior numbers of Rebels and forced to withdraw.

Carr finally ordered a general retreat when the swarming Confederates threatened to engulf his command. The Union troops steadily fell back through thick woods on either side of Telegraph Road, fending off repeated Confederate attacks. About a half-mile south of the tavern Carr regrouped his command along the south side of Benjamin Ruddick's cornfield and made another stand.

In the deepening twilight Van Dorn finally emerged from Cross Timber Hollow onto the high ground atop Pea Ridge. A

few hundred yards south of the tavern he reached the inter-
section with Ford Road. The perplexed Confederate commander searched to the west but there was no sign of McCulloch's
Division. With only half of the Army of the West on hand for
what seemed to be the climactic moment of the battle, Van
Dorn nonetheless decided to make a final effort to sweep away
the stubborn Federals and win the day. With darkness rapidly
enveloping the field, there was no time for the Confederates to
reconnoiter or reorganize. Van Dorn ordered an immediate
frontal assault against Carr's position.

Unseen by the Confederates in the gloom, Curtis arrived on
the field personally leading hundreds of fresh troops and additional cannon to bolster Carr's weary, rattled men. Shortly
afterward the ill-fated Confederate assault began. A disorganized mass of Price's Missourians—perhaps 3,000 men—
surged across the cornfield directly toward the Union line.
Vinson Holman of the 9th Iowa was startled to hear "their
cheers and yells rising above the roar of artillery." Such gallantry counted for little as blasts of canister from cannon lined
up wheel to wheel slaughtered the oncoming Rebels. "By this
time it was almost dark," remembered Asa Payne, "and we got
so near the battery that the fire from the guns would pass in
jetting streams through our lines." The ghastly affair was over
in fifteen minutes. Badly shaken survivors of the doomed
assault streamed back toward the woods surrounding Elkhorn
Tavern while the Federals cheered and jeered in triumph.
Darkness soon brought an end to the fighting. The unsuccessful attack in Ruddick's Field late on March 7 was the high
water mark of the Confederate effort at Pea Ridge. Henceforth,
Curtis would control the course of the battle.

During the day Curtis gradually realized that he had underestimated Van Dorn's audacity. By mid-afternoon he finally
concluded that the entire Confederate army had gotten around
his right flank and was moving into his rear. While fighting
raged at Leetown and Elkhorn Tavern he carried out a com-

plete 180-degree change of front from south to north, gradually shifting his combat units northward from the Little Sugar
Creek fortifications to the broad plateau of Pea Ridge, and, at
the same time, moving his massive supply trains southward
out of harm's way. It was an enormously complicated under-
taking unparalleled in the Civil War. During the night of March
7-8, Curtis again demonstrated his mastery of staff work by
using interior lines to consolidate the Army of the Southwest.
He abandoned the Little Sugar Creek position entirely and
moved all of his scattered forces, including the victorious
troops at Leetown, to reinforce Carr's battered division strad-
dling Telegraph Road. He also distributed food, water, and
ammunition. By dawn on March 8 the Union army was ready
for a second day of battle.

Van Dorn attempted to do the same with the Army of the
West. He ordered Greer to gather up the fragments of
McCulloch's Division at Leetown and join him at Elkhorn
Tavern. Greer dutifully led his skeletal command on an all-
night march around Big Mountain on the Bentonville Detour,
but the troops arrived in such pitiful condition as to be almost
useless. The Confederates around the tavern were without food
except for what was found in Federal haversacks and sutlers'
wagons. They also were without adequate ammunition, for in
the confusion of the march along the Bentonville Detour the
previous night, the supply train had been left behind a dozen
miles distant in Little Sugar Creek valley. No one at
Confederate headquarters knew where the train was, and no
one thought to begin a search until the next morning. Van
Dorn's failure to organize a proper staff before launching the
campaign now began to take its toll.

Dawn broke on March 8 and Curtis waited to see if Van
Dorn would continue to press his attack. When nothing happened, Curtis concluded that the Confederates had shot their
bolt and that he now held the initiative. He formed the entire
Army of the Southwest into a curved line of battle that strad-

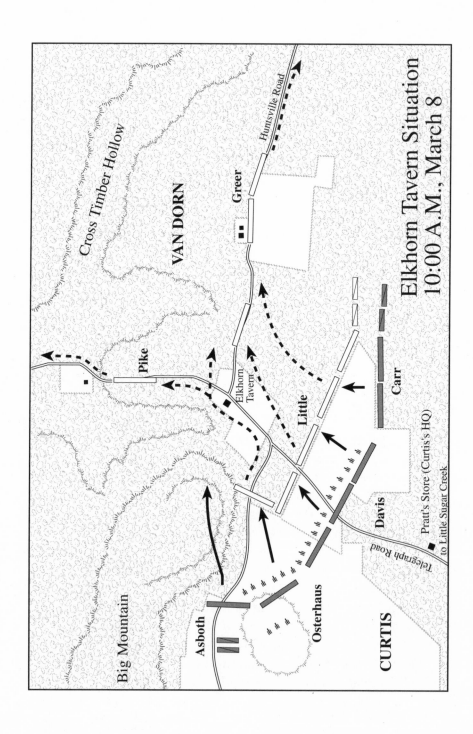

Elkhorn Tavern Situation
10:00 A.M., March 8

dled Telegraph Road and faced Elkhorn Tavern. The Union line was more than a mile in length. Then he ordered his artillery to wheel forward. For two hours dozens of Union cannon hammered the Confederates at ever closer ranges. It was the most intense field artillery bombardment of the Civil War up to that time and it mightily impressed those who were present. According to Leach Clark, a soldier in the 36th Illinois, "the constant roar of artillery seemed to shake the ground like an earthquake." Captain Cummings of the 4th Iowa was at a loss for words and simply told his wife: "It was the grandest thing I ever saw or thought of." The tremendous noise could be heard over fifty miles away in Springfield and Fayetteville.

The devastation wrought on the Confederates was terrible. Outgunned and low on ammunition, Van Dorn's artillery was wrecked or driven from the field and his infantry was forced to seek shelter deep in the woods. Under cover of the bombardment Union infantry moved ever nearer to the Confederate position.

A member of Curtis's staff observed that during the cannonade the Union commander behaved "about as calmly and with as much composure as if overseeing a farm." Around 10 A.M. Curtis halted the bombardment and casually said to Sigel: "General, I think the infantry might advance now." As orders passed down the chain of command, nearly 10,000 Federal soldiers dressed ranks and aligned on units to their right and left. It was the only time in the Civil War that an entire army—infantry, cavalry, and artillery—was visible in line of battle from flank to flank. Surgeon Gordon of the 18th Indiana spoke for many when he described the imposing martial array as "the grandest sight that I had ever beheld."

As drums rolled and bugles rang, the curving blue line swept across the woods and fields atop Pea Ridge, converging on Elkhorn Tavern from the west and south. "That beautiful charge I shall never forget," wrote Captain Eugene B. Payne of the 37th Illinois. "With banners streaming, with drums beat-

Battle of Pea Ridge, March 8, 1862

ing, and our long line of blue coats advancing upon the double quick, with their deadly bayonets gleaming in the sunlight, and every man and officer yelling at the top of his lungs. The rebel yell was nowhere in comparison." Confederate opposition was scattered and ineffective because of the shattering impact of the bombardment.

Van Dorn realized that his position was hopeless and ordered an immediate withdrawal. The retreat rapidly degenerated into a rout after Van Dorn and Price rode away to the east on Huntsville Road, leaving thousands of Confederate soldiers still engaged. Many Rebels concluded, with good reason, that they had been abandoned by their leaders and fled in all directions. While the Confederates scrambled to get away, the soldiers of the Army of the Southwest rapidly recovered all the ground lost the previous day. Curtis rode up Telegraph Road behind his advancing line, enthralled by the fierce grandeur of battle. "A charge of infantry like that last closing scene has never been made on this continent," he later told his brother. "It was the most terribly magnificent sight that can be imagined." At Elkhorn Tavern Curtis shook hands with Sigel, then rode among his wildly cheering men, waving his hat and shouting "Victory! Victory!"

Because the dissolving Army of the West escaped on three different roads leading north, east, and west, Curtis was unable to organize an effective pursuit. Instead he scoured the countryside for Rebel stragglers, collected wagonloads of discarded weapons and equipment, and settled down to care for the wounded of both armies. The latter task was particularly difficult because of the paucity of adequate medical facilities, personnel, and supplies in a frontier region. When Curtis finally learned for certain that the Confederates were streaming away in retreat, he sent a courier racing north with a message for Halleck in St. Louis: "Indiana, Illinois, Iowa, Ohio, and Missouri very proudly share the honor of victory which their gallant heroes won over the combined forces of Van Dorn,

Price, and McCulloch at Pea Ridge, in the Ozark Mountains of Arkansas." Missouri was safe for the foreseeable future.

The Union triumph did not come cheap. Pea Ridge cost the Federals 1,384 casualties: 203 killed, 980 wounded, and 201 missing, approximately 13 percent of the 10,250 troops engaged in the battle. Confederate casualties are less certain because Van Dorn lied—and lied inconsistently—about his losses. The Army of the West consisted of well over 16,000 men at the outset of the campaign, but suffered serious attrition en route to Pea Ridge. A conservative estimate is that the Confederates lost at least 2,000 of the 12,000 to 13,000 troops engaged in the battle, a casualty rate of roughly 15 percent.

The Confederate retreat from Pea Ridge was even more disastrous than the advance. Late on the evening of March 8 most of the Army of the West reassembled at Van Winkle's Mill southeast of the battlefield. The famished men and animals devoured everything in sight, but the sparsely populated Ozark countryside provided only a fraction of the food and forage necessary to feed such a hungry horde. "I never knew what it was to want for something to eat until the last fifteen days," Tom Coleman of the 11th Texas Cavalry confided to his parents. Samuel B. Barron of the 3rd Texas Cavalry believed he was "in much greater danger of dying from starvation in the mountains of northern Arkansas than by the enemy's bullets." For the next week the pathetic column staggered south on primitive trails, generally moving up the narrowing valley of the White River.

Hundreds of Rebels wandered away in search of food and never returned to the ranks. The trail of the defeated army was littered with discarded clothing, weapons, pots and pans, and even flags. The Confederates did not return to their original camps in the Boston Mountains but continued south to the Arkansas River. By the time they finally reached Van Buren, they were a pitiful remnant of the proud army that had opened the campaign two weeks earlier.

While his troops recuperated, Van Dorn received a telegram from General P. G. T. Beauregard, who strongly suggested that Van Dorn move his command to Corinth, Mississippi, as part of a concentration of all Confederate armies west of the Appalachian Mountains. The purpose of this grand design was to defeat General Ulysses S. Grant's Union army camped at Pittsburg Landing on the Tennessee River. Van Dorn agreed and began to shift his force eastward from Van Buren. Heavy spring rains slowed the march and the troops did not begin boarding steamboats until April 6. By then it was too late. The battle of Shiloh was underway—a battle the Confederacy might have won had Van Dorn's thousands of soldiers and dozens of cannon been present.

Van Dorn did more than merely transfer his army from one side of the Mississippi River to the other—he all but abandoned Arkansas and Missouri. Acting on his own authority, Van Dorn carried away nearly all troops, weapons, equipment, stores, machinery, and animals in the vast area under his command. One can only wonder whether Van Dorn understood the political and military ramifications of his amazingly cavalier actions. With the Army of the West now in Mississippi, and with outraged Arkansas political leaders appealing for help, Beauregard assigned command of the denuded District of the Trans-Mississippi to Major General Thomas C. Hindman, a prominent Arkansas politician. Hindman arrived in Little Rock at the end of May and was shocked. "I found here almost nothing," he complained. "Nearly everything of value was taken away by General Van Dorn." The fiery Hindman was undaunted, however, and he set out to restore Confederate military strength west of the Mississippi River.

When Curtis learned that Van Dorn was moving down the Arkansas River, he also shifted eastward in order to protect Missouri's vulnerable southern flank. For several weeks the Union army struggled across the rugged central portion of the Ozark Plateau. By the end of April Curtis knew that Van Dorn had crossed into Mississippi, so he again turned south and drove into north-central Arkansas. The Army of the Southwest was hampered by enormous logistical difficulties, but Curtis came within fifty miles of Little Rock before the overland sup-

Thomas C. Hindman: born Tennessee 1828; Hindman moved with his family to Mississippi in 1841; he studied for a time at the Classical Institute in New Jersey, but with the onset of the Mexican War he returned to Mississippi to help raise a company for volunteer service; he served as a lieutenant in Mexico and returned to Mississippi to practice law; in 1854 he was elected to the Mississippi legislature, and served one term; in 1856 he relocated to Helena, Arkansas, where he practiced law and was elected in 1858 to the U.S. House of Representatives; reelected in 1860, he instead resigned from Congress upon Arkansas' withdrawal from the

Union in April 1861; he organized the 2d Arkansas Infantry and was elected its colonel; after service in central Kentucky, during which he was made a brigadier general, Hindman commanded a division in the Battle of Shiloh in April 1862; promoted to major general, he returned to Arkansas to command the Trans-Mississippi District and the District of Arkansas, but his harsh measures there caused his removal from command in August 1862; commanding the First Corps of the Trans-Mississippi Department, Hindman was defeated at Prairie Grove in December; thereafter he transferred to the Army of Tennessee and commanded a division in General James Longstreet's wing in the September 1863 Confederate victory at Chickamauga, in which he remained on the field despite a painful wound; returning to duty in December, he assumed command of the corps formerly headed by General John C. Breckinridge; superseded by General John

B. Hood in March 1864, Hindman, although quite displeased, commanded a division in Hood's Corps in the early stages of the Atlanta Campaign; a wound to the eye incapacitated him for the remainder of the war; he moved to Mexico following the conflict but returned to Helena in 1867; an outspoken critic of Arkansas' Reconstruction government, General Hindman was murdered in his home by unknown gunmen in 1868.

ply route from Missouri reached the breaking point. Efforts to create an alternate waterborne supply route via the Mississippi and White Rivers failed. Curtis veered away from Little Rock and turned east toward the Mississippi River where his little army could rest and refit. Along the way he brushed aside several feeble Confederate attempts to bar his path. The largest such engagement occurred on July 6 at Cache River, near Cotton Plant. It was a one-sided affair that resulted in the deaths of 6 Union soldiers and up to 136 Confederate soldiers. On July 12 the weary Union soldiers entered Helena, finally bringing the long campaign to a close.

The Pea Ridge campaign was one of the most remarkable operations of the Civil War. During the first six months of 1862, the Army of the Southwest marched over seven hundred miles across difficult terrain and fought and won a major battle against imposing odds. Halleck and Curtis achieved their major strategic objectives of securing Missouri and freeing scarce resources for use elsewhere. From the Union perspective, the campaign was a major success. Exactly the opposite was true from the Confederate perspective. Van Dorn, McCulloch, and Price failed to recover Missouri or defend Arkansas. When the Pea Ridge campaign ended in the summer of 1862, most of Missouri was securely in Union hands, much of Arkansas was lost to the Confederacy, and the balance of power in the Trans-Mississippi was dramatically altered. Both sides now had to deal with this dramatic shift in fortunes.

6
CONFEDERATE RESURGENCE

Even before Curtis and his men tramped into Helena, Hindman was busy creating a new Confederate military structure to fill the void left behind by Van Dorn. Hindman was a fanatic who did not intend to allow public opinion or constitutional rights to stand in the way of Southern independence. He declared martial law on his own authority, restricted civilian travel, rigorously enforced the unpopular Conscription Act, and executed deserters. He commandeered all Texas troops passing through Arkansas en route to Tennessee or Virginia and obtained the return of a division of Price's troops (though not Price himself) from Mississippi. He set prices for food and other consumer goods and established shops to manufacture arms, ammunition, and equipment. Finally, he authorized the formation of "Partisan Rangers" to harass Federal supply lines. (These packs of unsupervised irregulars soon degenerated into roving criminal gangs that murdered hundreds if not thousands of soldiers and civilians in Arkansas, Missouri, and the Indian Territory during the remaining three years of the war, but Hindman was long gone by then.)

By the fall of 1862 the abrasive, hard-driving Hindman had created an embryonic army and a rudimentary logistical base in the least populous and least developed part of the Confederacy. Hindman's draconian actions produced results but also triggered massive disaffection. President Davis recognized that a lighter touch was needed and appointed

Theophilus H. Holmes: born North Carolina 1804; Holmes was graduated from the U.S. Military Academy in 1829, forty-fourth in his class of forty-six; he served on the frontier and against the Seminoles in Florida; brevetted for gallantry in the Mexican War, he rose through the ranks to major; he resigned his commission in

April 1861 to enter Confederate service; appointed brigadier general in June, he commanded the Department of Fredericksburg and was present, though not engaged, at First Manassas; promoted to major general, he headed the Aquia District, Department of Northern Virginia, from October 1861 to March 1862, and the Department of North Carolina from March to July 1862; he commanded a division and performed poorly during the Seven Days' Battles; dispatched to the West, he commanded the Trans-Mississippi Department from July 1862 to March 1863, when he was superseded by General E. Kirby Smith; having been promoted to lieutenant general in October 1862, he assumed direction of the District of Arkansas, a command he held until relieved in March 1864; he spent the last year of the war in command of reserve forces in North Carolina; after the war he engaged in farming near Fayetteville, North Carolina, and died at his home there in 1880. Seriously deaf, General Holmes was unfit for field command and, by his own admission, lacked the ability to command a large department; his lofty rank and appointments owed more to his friendship with Jefferson Davis than to any demonstrated ability.

Lieutenant General Theophilus H. Holmes to command the troubled region, now upgraded to the Department of the Trans-Mississippi. Holmes was an aging, timid, vacillating officer known derisively to his men as "Granny." He reached Little Rock in August and retained Hindman as his principal subordinate and field commander, probably because he valued the younger man's drive and determination.

Holmes and Hindman were very different personalities and they held very different views about the military situation west of the Mississippi River. Holmes preferred a passive defensive strategy that he hoped would discourage the Federals from overrunning more of Arkansas and the Indian Territory; Hindman believed the department could best be defended by pursuing an aggressive offensive strategy that would rock the Federals back on their heels and permit the Rebels to recover lost ground in Arkansas, the Indian Territory, and even Missouri. Like Price and Van Dorn before him, Hindman saw Missouri as the key to Confederate success in the West. He desperately wanted "to push forward toward the Missouri River with the greatest vigor" and carry the war to the enemy. Holmes characteristically feared that such a move would annoy the Federals and provoke them into launching an offensive toward Little Rock.

Since the beginning of 1862 the Confederates had only reacted to Union moves in the Trans-Mississippi, but Hindman convinced Holmes to allow him to regain lost territory in northwestern Arkansas and southwestern Missouri. In other words, Hindman intended to restore the strategic situation that had existed atop the Ozark Plateau before the Pea Ridge campaign. Holmes appointed Hindman commander of the rather awkwardly named First Corps of the Army of the Trans-Mississippi. During the fall Hindman struggled to feed, shelter, train, and equip the raw recruits and unwilling conscripts who trickled into his headquarters at Fort Smith. Progress was slow because almost everything—food, tents, clothing, equipment, wagons, draft animals, arms, and ammunition—was in short supply. The South's limited industrial base, its primitive transportation system (especially west of the Mississippi), and the geographical location of Fort Smith on the frontier all combined to make life difficult for the men of the First Corps. "We have in our Regiment no conveniences of any kind scarcely," complained an Arkansas soldier named David W. Moore. "No tents, no clothing, no cooking utensils and in fact scarcely anything have been issued by the Government to the men." It was the same in every regiment. Lieutenant Pleasant M. Cox of the 9th Missouri succinctly described the army to his parents. "They are," he wrote, "the ragedist lot of men that I ever saw."

John M. Schofield: born New York 1831; Schofield was graduated from the U.S. Military Academy in 1853, seventh in his class of fifty-two that included John B. Hood, Philip H. Sheridan, and James B. McPherson; commissioned 2d lieutenant and assigned to artillery, he served on garrison duty in Florida and taught at West Point; promoted to 1st lieutenant, he took a leave of absence to teach physics at Washington University in St. Louis; he was promoted to captain, 1st Artillery, in

1861, and entered the Civil War as a major in the 1st Missouri Infantry, a regiment he later reorganized as the 1st Missouri Light Artillery; he served on the staff of General Nathaniel Lyon during the capture of Camp Jackson and in the Battle of Wilson's Creek, for which he earned the Medal of Honor; promoted to brigadier general, U.S. Volunteers in November 1861, he commanded the District of St. Louis and the Missouri Militia; after a succession of district commands, he was appointed major general, U.S.V., in November 1862, and commanded the Army of the Frontier until March 1863, when his appointment to major general lapsed for lack of Senate confirmation; he briefly headed a division in the Army of the Cumberland, but in May 1863 was reappointed and confirmed as major general to rank from November 1862; he commanded the Department of Missouri until

After months of wrestling with seemingly insoluble administrative and logistical problems, Hindman grew impatient to get underway. This led him to make an error in judgment. He sent several detachments of Confederate cavalry into southwestern Missouri to harass the Union garrisons at Springfield and nearby towns. These ill-conceived raids accomplished little except to alert Curtis, who had succeeded Halleck as commander of the Department of the Missouri, to the fact that the Rebels once again were threatening Union control of Missouri. Curtis had swept Price's army out of southwestern Missouri eight months earlier, and he was determined to prevent the Confederates from reestablishing themselves in that region.

February 1864, when he assumed command of the Department and Army of Ohio; he led his army, the Twenty-third Corps, throughout General William T. Sherman's Atlanta Campaign; after that city's fall, Schofield was dispatched to oppose Hood's invasion of Tennessee; after escaping disaster at Spring Hill, he fought Hood at Franklin in November 1864; although not victorious, his force severely mauled the Confederates; he then led the Twenty-third Corps under General George H. Thomas in the rout of Hood's army at Nashville; elevated directly from captain to brigadier general in the regular army for his efforts in Tennessee, Schofield moved with his corps to North Carolina to participate in Sherman's final offensive; at the close of the war he was in command of the Department of North Carolina; brevetted major general, U.S.A., he was sent to France to negotiate an end to the French intervention in Mexico; continuing in the regular army, he served as Secretary of War from 1868 to 1869, during which time he recommended the acquisition of Pearl Harbor as a naval base; returning to active duty following the inauguration of U.S. Grant in 1869, he was elevated to major general; he served as superintendent of West Point from 1876 to 1881, and presided in the Fitz John Porter case; in 1888 he succeeded Sheridan as commanding general of the army; promoted to lieutenant general in 1895, he was retired later that year by operation of the law on his sixty-fourth birthday; General Schofield died at St. Augustine, Florida, in 1906. Despite his relative lack of combat experience, Schofield performed credibly in the latter stages of the war; the fact that he did so under Sherman's command largely accounted for his promotion over several more senior and, arguably, more deserving officers; throughout his post-war career, Schofield was a tireless advocate of military reforms.

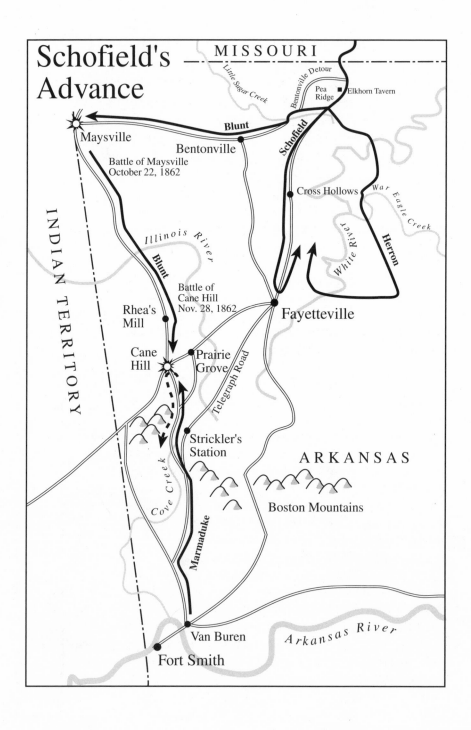

Schofield's Advance

MISSOURI

Little Sugar Creek

Bentonville Detour

Pea Ridge

Elkhorn Tavern

Blunt

Schofield

Maysville

Bentonville

Battle of Maysville October 22, 1862

Cross Hollows

War Eagle Creek

White River

Herron

INDIAN TERRITORY

Illinois River

Blunt

Battle of Cane Hill Nov. 28, 1862

Rhea's Mill

Fayetteville

Cane Hill

Prairie Grove

Telegraph Road

Cove Creek

Strickler's Station

ARKANSAS

Marmaduke

Boston Mountains

Van Buren

Arkansas River

Fort Smith

Curtis directed his principal subordinate, Brigadier General John M. Schofield, to clean out the Rebels. Schofield gathered together a force that he called the Army of the Frontier and set out for Springfield. Schofield was eager for military glory, but during several weeks of campaigning in southwestern Missouri he demonstrated only a modest capacity for field command. Nevertheless, after a sharp clash at Newtonia, northwest of Springfield, on October 4, Schofield finally prevailed by sheer weight of numbers and pushed the scattered Confederate

James G. Blunt: born Maine 1826; after several years at sea, Blunt was graduated from a medical school in Columbus, Ohio; he practiced medicine in Ohio and in 1856 removed to Kansas; a staunch abolitionist and associate of John Brown, Blunt became involved in Kansas politics; at the outbreak of the Civil War, he was a lieutenant colonel in James H. Lane's irregular Kansas Brigade; commissioned a brigadier general of U.S. Volunteers in April 1862, he commanded the Department of Kansas from May to September of that year; commanding the First Division, Army of the Frontier, he defeated General Douglas Cooper's Confederate Indians at Old Fort Wayne and General John Marmaduke's command at Cain Hill; he joined General Francis J. Herron in the defeat of General Thomas C. Hindman's Confederates at Prairie Grove in December 1862 and subsequently captured Van Buren, Arkansas; promoted to major general of volunteers, he again defeated Cooper's Indians in July 1863 at Honey Springs, Indian Territory; he headed the District of the Frontier from June 1863 to January 1864; while commanding the District of Upper Arkansas, July through December 1864, he participated in the repulse of General Sterling Price's Missouri Raid; he commanded the District of South Kansas during the final months of the war and mustered out in July 1865; after the war he practiced medicine in Leavenworth, Kansas, and worked for several years as a government claims agent in Washington, D.C.; he died at Washington in 1881, having been institutionalized for insanity during the last years of his life.

detachments back into Arkansas and the Indian Territory.

Without any particular strategic objective in mind, Schofield led his command into northwestern Arkansas on October 18. The Army of the Frontier camped on the Pea Ridge battleground, then occupied Fayetteville, Bentonville, and Cross Hollows. On October 22 a division led by Brigadier General James G. Blunt routed a small force of Confederate Indians at Old Fort Wayne in the Indian Territory, just west of Maysville, Arkansas. By the end of October all of the Confederate detachments sent into Missouri had fallen back across the Boston Mountains to Fort Smith, and Union forces once again were spreading out across northwestern Arkansas. Hindman's initial attempt to rattle the Yankees and loosen their grip on southwestern Missouri had gone badly awry.

By the fall of 1862 the frontier settlements scattered across the Ozark Plateau in Missouri, Arkansas, and the Indian Territory had experienced the hard hand of war for nearly eighteen months. Foraging armies and rampaging guerrillas had stolen and slaughtered livestock, plundered and burned homes and barns and outbuildings, and murdered hundreds—perhaps even thousands—of inhabitants. Hundreds of farms and dozens of small towns had been abandoned. Many soldiers in the Trans-Mississippi were struck by the uncomfortable thought that their "civilized" warfare was just as brutal and merciless as the "savage" warfare practiced by Indians. Food production in the devastated and depopulated landscape dropped precipitously and foraging grew less productive with every passing month. Commanders on both sides discovered that maintaining a sizable army in the burned-out frontier region was an extremely difficult proposition.

Schofield was hampered by logistical problems at least as severe as those faced by Curtis. Early in November he concluded—prematurely, as it turned out—that the campaign was over. He withdrew to Springfield with two divisions, but left Blunt's Division in the northwestern corner of Arkansas near

Maysville where it could be supplied without too much difficulty across the prairie from Fort Scott, Kansas. Schofield soon became ill and returned to St. Louis. While recuperating he spent much of his time angling for a suitable position east of the Mississippi River, where greater glory presumably was to

Francis J. Herron: born Pennsylvania 1837; after attending the University of Pittsburg, Herron moved to Dubuque, Iowa, to engage in banking; active in the local militia company, the Governor's Grays, he offered his company's services to Abraham Lincoln prior to the president-elect's inauguration; with the outbreak of the Civil War, Herron entered the volunteer army as a captain in the 1st Iowa Infantry; he led his company at Wilson's Creek and was promoted to lieutenant colonel, 9th Iowa, in September 1861; he performed with conspicuous gallantry in the Battle of Pea Ridge, in which he was wounded and captured; exchanged shortly thereafter he was promoted to brigadier general U.S. Volunteers in July 1862; he was given command of the Third Division, Army of the Frontier, in October 1862;

that December he force-marched his division some 125 miles to relieve the beleaguered command of General James G. Blunt in Arkansas, where he joined Blunt in defeating General Thomas C. Hindman's Confederates at Prairie Grove; he was promoted to major general in March 1863, becoming at the time, the youngest major general in either army at the age of twenty-six; after briefly heading the Army of the Frontier, Herron and his division moved to Mississippi to participate in the final stages of the Vicksburg Campaign; transferring to the Department of the Gulf, Herron commanded U.S. forces in Texas and held various district commands in Louisiana; he headed the District of Northern Louisiana in the final months of the war and, after an assignment to negotiate treaties

with the Indians, he resigned his commission in June 1865; after the war he was a lawyer in Reconstruction Louisiana and served as that state's U.S. marshal and acting secretary of state; with the end of Federal occupation, Herron moved to New York, where he engaged in manufacturing; in 1893 he was awarded the Medal of Honor for Pea Ridge; he died in poverty at New York in 1902.

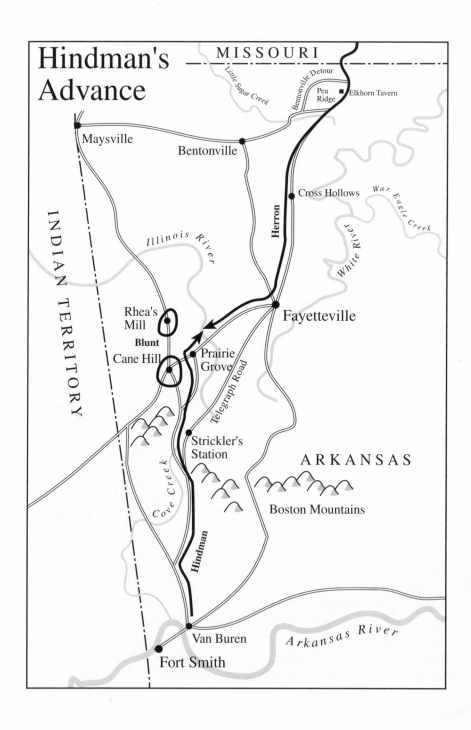

Hindman's Advance

MISSOURI

Little Sugar Creek

Bentonville Detour

Pea Ridge

■ Elkhorn Tavern

Maysville

Bentonville

Cross Hollows

War Eagle Creek

INDIAN TERRITORY

Illinois River

Herron

White River

Rhea's Mill

Fayetteville

Blunt

Cane Hill

Prairie Grove

Telegraph Road

Strickler's Station

ARKANSAS

Cove Creek

Boston Mountains

Hindman

Van Buren

Arkansas River

Fort Smith

be found. Schofield's illness and his preoccupation with promotion and position precluded him from exercising effective supervision over his army.

Command of the dispersed Army of the Frontier passed to Blunt, an abolitionist and aggressive amateur soldier who saw no reason to defer to his distant (and silent) commander in St. Louis. Emboldened by his success at Maysville and the withdrawal of Confederate forces beyond the Boston Mountains, Blunt led his isolated division south down the Military Road that ran along the border between Arkansas and the Indian Territory. The other two Federal divisions, commanded by Brigadier General Francis J. Herron of Pea Ridge fame, remained south of Springfield. By the end of November the main components of the Army of the Frontier were dangerously far apart. Curtis noticed this alarming development and repeatedly suggested to Blunt that he should pull back, but the headstrong Blunt ignored the advice.

Hindman was dismayed that his initial movement into Missouri had failed, but his spirits rose when he learned of the inviting disposition of the Army of the Frontier. Like Van Dorn nine months earlier, Hindman saw a glittering opportunity to defeat a Union army in detail and, perhaps, sweep into Missouri. He decided to attempt to cross the Boston Mountains undetected and overwhelm Blunt's isolated division before Herron could react. Back in Little Rock, Holmes was discomfited when he heard of Hindman's bold plan to march north and smite the Yankees, but grudgingly gave his permission.

The initial phase of the Confederate offensive did not go as planned, which should have been a caution to Hindman. Brigadier General John S. Marmaduke led a cavalry force of about 2,000 men across the Boston Mountains to distract Blunt and to screen Hindman's advance. To Marmaduke's surprise, Blunt rushed forward to meet him with a force of 5,000 men. The two unequal columns collided on November 28 at

Cane Hill and skirmished for nine hours across twelve miles of forested ridges and valleys. At the end of the day the Confederates retired into the Boston Mountains and repulsed a Federal pursuit. As was often the case in the Civil War when

John Sappington Marmaduke: born Missouri 1833; attended both Yale and Harvard before entering the U.S. Military Academy, graduating in 1857, thirtieth in his class of thirty-eight; commissioned 2d lieutenant and posted to infantry, he participated in the Mormon Expedition; still on frontier duty at the outbreak of the Civil War, he resigned his commission to become colonel in the Missouri state militia; fought at Boonville in 1861, but resigned his state commission to enter Confederate Service; commissioned 1st lieutenant; named lieutenant colonel of the 1st Arkansas Infantry Battalion; promoted to colonel, 3rd Confederate Infantry; wounded in an outstanding performance at Shiloh in April 1862; transferred to the

Trans-Mississippi, he commanded the cavalry in General T.C. Hindman's Corps, Army of the West; brigadier general November 1862; led a cavalry division that raided twice into Missouri; fought at Helena and Little Rock; he dueled with and killed fellow Confederate General Lucius Walker at Little Rock in September 1863, for which he was arrested but soon released; during the Red River Campaign in the spring of 1864 Marmaduke's cavalry, with General Samuel Bell Maxey's Texans and Indians, opposed General Frederick Steele's Arkansas operations at Poison Springs and Jenkins' Ferry; that fall he commanded a cavalry division in General Sterling Price's Missouri invasion; in November he was captured while directing a rear guard action in Kansas; imprisoned at Fort Warren, Massachusetts, for the remainder of the war, he was nonetheless promoted to major general in March 1865, becoming the last Confederate officer to be elevated to that rank; released from prison in July 1865; he worked in the insurance business after the war and edited an agricultural journal in Missouri; elected governor of that state in 1884; General Marmaduke died in office in 1887. He was a gifted cavalry commander whose efforts largely escaped recognition outside the isolated Trans-Mississippi.

mounted forces were engaged, casualties were light: the Federals lost nine killed, thirty-two wounded, and a small number missing; Confederate losses probably were slightly higher.

A crestfallen Marmaduke withdrew across the Boston Mountains before Hindman could ferry the main body of the First Corps across the Arkansas River from Fort Smith to Van Buren. Hindman was not particularly upset, however, when he realized that the engagement at Cane Hill had drawn Blunt thirty-five miles deeper into Arkansas. Blunt's lone division now was located at the northern edge of the Boston Mountains, over one hundred miles from Herron's two divisions near Springfield, but only thirty miles from Hindman's army at Van Buren. Blunt was more vulnerable than ever and Hindman believed it was imperative that the Confederates take advantage of this extraordinary opportunity.

7
RETURN OF THE ARMIES

On December 3, the First Corps of the Army of the Trans-Mississippi left Van Buren and headed north toward the Boston Mountains. Hindman's 12,000 men and 31 cannon exemplified Van Dorn's crippling legacy to the Confederacy west of the Mississippi. The First Corps was impressive on paper, but in reality it was a makeshift army cobbled together and rushed into battle without adequate training and equipment. Some men were veterans but most were untried in battle, and many were conscripts of uncertain reliability. They were armed with a reasonably effective mix of rifles, smoothbores, and shotguns, but they carried only enough ammunition for a single day of combat. The artillery was light and unimpressive. Draft animals were emaciated due to a lack of forage, and the small number of wagons that composed the rickety train could not support the army in the field for more than a week.

Hindman was determined to succeed despite the obvious

weaknesses in his command. His plan was simple. Marmaduke would advance across the Boston Mountains once again and create a diversion by threatening Cane Hill from the south. With Blunt's attention fixed on Marmaduke, Hindman and the main body of the First Corps would swing around Blunt's left flank and strike him from the east. The single Union division would be overwhelmed on the spot or be driven into the wilderness of the Indian Territory, where it would be without possibility of reinforcement and would have to withdraw into Kansas.

Blunt was stubborn and pugnacious but he was no fool. He knew that his advanced position practically invited an attack, so he kept a close watch on Confederate activity in his front. Union scouts—many of them Indians—reported that something was afoot the day before Hindman marched out of Van Buren. Blunt assumed correctly that he was the target and ordered Herron to march immediately to his support. Despite the gravity of the situation, Blunt did not fall back toward Missouri to meet Herron halfway, as Curtis had been urging for weeks. "I have decided to hold on at all hazards," he announced, though there was no important tactical or strategic reason for doing so. Blunt placed his troops in defensive positions around Cane Hill and prepared for a fight. The decision to stand and fight at Cane Hill was a mistake that nearly led to disaster. "Blunt was a hearty fighter and seemed to think that it was the height of strategy to get himself surrounded by the enemy and fight his way out," remarked an exasperated Union soldier. Indeed, Blunt did seem to enjoy his predicament. As Hindman crept ever closer, Blunt notified Fort Scott of the situation, adding: "You will soon hear of one of the damnedest fights or foot races that has taken place lately."

For three days Blunt anxiously waited for the Confederates to emerge from the Boston Mountains. On December 6, Marmaduke's cavalry finally appeared and clashed with the Union cavalry screen south of Cane Hill. While this noisy diversion was in progress, Hindman led a slow-moving column of infantry and artillery around to the east of Cane Hill. The Confederates were hampered by fatigue, primitive roads, and failing draft animals. Nevertheless, events generally were unfolding according to plan, if not on schedule. Then, during the night of December 6-7, Hindman learned that Herron had left Springfield and was hastening down Telegraph Road to Blunt's relief.

Hindman had not expected the Yankees to discover his movements so soon or to react so quickly. He realized he could not attack Blunt from the east as originally planned, for this would expose his own rear to Herron, whose strength and progress were not known. Hindman decided instead to continue moving around Cane Hill and intercept Herron somewhere well to the northeast of Blunt's position. After defeating Herron, the First Corps would turn back and deal with Blunt.

Hindman's hastily revised plan was seriously flawed. It required the Confederates to march farther and faster than originally anticipated and ignored the fact that they did not have enough ammunition to fight two battles, one against Herron and another against Blunt. Perhaps even worse, the plan allowed Blunt potential freedom of action. It was essential that Marmaduke's cavalry division lead the way north in order to halt Herron as far away from Cane Hill as possible. This meant, of course, that Marmaduke no longer would be able to bluff the Union troops into staying put at Cane Hill. It would be only a matter of time before Blunt began to stir.

Despite misgivings, Hindman and the First Corps struck out across the rolling terrain east of Cane Hill the next morning, December 7. The weary men and animals made slow progress and straggling was epidemic. Shortly after sunrise Marmaduke's Division, with Colonel Joseph O. Shelby's brigade in the lead, encountered the 1st Arkansas (Union) Cavalry near the Illinois River, about halfway between Cane Hill and Fayetteville. The surprised Arkansans (known as "Mountain

Feds" because nearly all lived atop the Ozark Plateau and had little enthusiasm for slavery or secession) were routed and fled back to Fayetteville in great disorder. The Confederates pursued, bagging hundreds of prisoners, until they were

Joseph O. Shelby: born Kentucky 1830; from a wealthy and influential family, Shelby attended Transylvania University in Kentucky and prospered in the hemp processing business; in 1852 he established a hemp plantation in Missouri and became one of that state's leading citizens; a slave owner and staunch pro-slavery advocate, Shelby became embroiled in "Bleeding Kansas" and the border wars of the mid-1850s; with the outbreak of the Civil War, he raised, financed, and led a cavalry company in Missouri's pro-Confederate state forces under General Sterling Price; he fought at Wilson's Creek and at Pea Ridge as well as in dozens of skirmishes; he raided extensively in Missouri in 1862, bringing in hundreds of recruits; commissioned into Confederate service that spring, he was promoted to colonel during the summer; he led a cavalry brigade in General Thomas Hindman's army during the Battle of Prairie Grove in December 1862, after which he took part in General John Marmaduke's Missouri raid; wounded in the attempted capture of Helena, Arkansas, in July 1863, he led a successful raid into Missouri that fall; promoted to brigadier general in December 1862, he performed admirably during operations against General Frederick Steele's Arkansas Campaign in the spring of 1864 and in Price's disastrous Missouri Raid that fall; refusing to surrender in 1865, Shelby led a highly romanticized Confederate exodus to Mexico, where he established a colony, Carlota, in the state of Veracruz; the Mexican adventure proved untenable and Shelby returned to Missouri in 1867; financially devastated by the war, he worked to reestablish himself but never regained his prewar stature; in 1883 he testified on behalf of Frank James during the outlaw's murder trial; appointed  U.S. marshal for the Western District of Missouri in 1893, he died at Adrian, Missouri, in 1897. A dashing figure, Shelby was no doubt a gifted commander; although he often attracted the assistance of such dubious elements as William C. Quantrill's bushwhackers, his "Iron Brigade" outperformed most mounted units in the Trans-Mississippi.

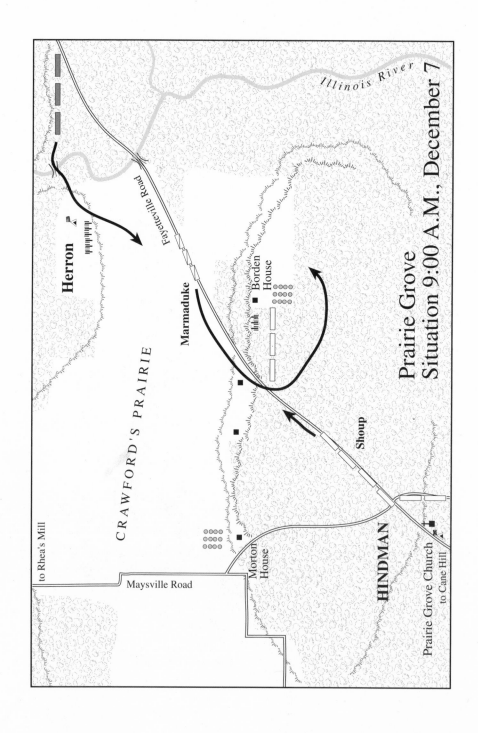

Prairie Grove
Situation 9:00 A.M., December 7

brought up short by the sight of a long blue column of cavalry, infantry, and artillery winding out of Fayetteville and heading in their direction.

Marmaduke was dumbfounded—and with good reason. The presence of Herron's two divisions at Fayetteville that morning was nothing short of miraculous. Herron had received Blunt's message late on December 3 and had placed his troops in motion early the next morning. The weather was mild and dry and Herron set a furious pace. During the next three days the Federals marched one hundred and ten miles—an average of almost thirty-five miles per day. Some units covered the final sixty-six miles in only thirty hours! The march was the most extraordinary event of its kind in the Civil War and an epic of human endurance. The pace of the march naturally caused serious attrition. Halfway through the ordeal, a Union soldier, too tired to engage in punctuation, noted in his diary that "our boys are laying along the road side every mile between this point and Springfield entirely disheartened completely exhausted can go no farther." About 7,000 Federal soldiers set out at the beginning but only about half that number were on their feet at the end. Herron's attenuated command reached Fayetteville during the night of December 6-7, halted for a brief rest, then moved on at sunrise and clashed with Marmaduke's cavalry.

Marmaduke fell back before the inexorable advance of Herron's weary, footsore infantry. About ten miles southwest of Fayetteville the road crossed the Illinois River and ascended a low hill surrounded by rolling grasslands. Most of the hill was covered with a thick growth of trees and a tangle of under-brush. In a small clearing near the center of the rise stood a modest structure known as Prairie Grove Presbyterian Church. Marmaduke halted atop the hill to await the arrival of Hindman's infantry and artillery, which slowly came up from the Boston Mountains. By this stage of the campaign the Confederates, too, had suffered considerable attrition, and the

First Corps probably consisted of no more than 11,000 men.

Hindman reached Prairie Grove at mid-morning. He intended to drive Herron's force back to Fayetteville, but his men trickled in so slowly he was compelled to assume a defensive posture. He deployed most of his infantry, dismounted cavalry, and artillery atop the hill in a semicircle facing north, directly

Daniel M. Frost: born New York 1823; Frost was graduated from the U.S. Military Academy in 1844, fourth in his class of twenty-five; commissioned a 2d lieutenant and posted to artillery, he later transferred to the Mounted Rifles; he served on the frontier and won a brevet during the Mexican War; after an assignment to Europe, Frost resigned from the army as a 1st lieutenant and settled at St.Louis, where he engaged in business, served in the Missouri legislature, and sat on the U.S.

Military Academy's Board of Visitors; a brigadier general of state troops at the outbreak of the Civil War, he was active in support of Missouri secession; in March 1861 he was compelled to surrender Camp Jackson to the Unionists under Nathaniel Lyon; exchanged, he joined General Sterling Price's army in southwest Missouri; he commanded Missouri state troops in the Battle of Pea Ridge, Arkansas, in March 1862, after which he raised an artillery brigade that he took across the Mississippi; at Corinth, he served briefly as General Braxton Bragg's inspector general; promoted to brigadier general, C.S.A., in October 1862, to rank from the previous March, Frost was returned to the Trans-Mississippi; he commanded a division in General Thomas C. Hindman's army at Prairie Grove, Arkansas, in December 1862; he commanded a division for much of 1863 and took part in the unsuccessful defense of Little Rock; in the fall of 1863, Frost left the army to join his family who had fled to Canada after being banished from their home near St.Louis; apparently Frost failed to submit a formal resignation or to receive authorization for a leave and was dropped from the army rolls in December 1863; after the war he returned to St. Louis County, where he engaged in farming until his death in 1900.

athwart the Fayetteville Road. Marmaduke's Division was on the right, Brigadier General Francis A. Shoup's Division was in the center on either side of the road, and Brigadier General Daniel M. Frost's Division was on the left. Hindman also kept a close watch to his rear, for Prairie Grove is only eight miles distant from Cane Hill.

Perhaps Hindman had an opportunity during the morning to mull over how his plans had gone awry because of Herron's alacrity and his unrealistic expectation of what his own army could accomplish. Now Hindman was between two Union forces whose combined strength was almost equal to his own. To make matters worse, Blunt and Herron were among the two most combative Union generals west of the Mississippi River. Hindman had hoped to push the Yankees out of Arkansas; now the survival of the Confederate army was in doubt.

8

THE BATTLE OF PRAIRIE GROVE

During the morning of December 7, Herron and his two shrunken divisions forded the Illinois River and deployed on Crawford's Prairie opposite the Confederate right atop Prairie Grove. Herron was outnumbered better than two to one. Moreover, the 3,500 or so men who were still with him were hardly in the best condition for a grueling fight. Undaunted, Herron ordered his four artillery batteries into action against the lighter Confederate artillery planted on the forward slope of the hill.

Around 10 A.M. the twenty-four Union cannon roared to life and began raining destruction on the Confederate position. "All this firing of artillery was incessant, and furious cannon shells, canister, and grape shot came flying all around us," recalled Spencer H. Mitchell, a Missouri Rebel in Parson's Brigade. The bombardment lasted two hours. By noon all of the Confederate cannon on Hindman's right had been disabled

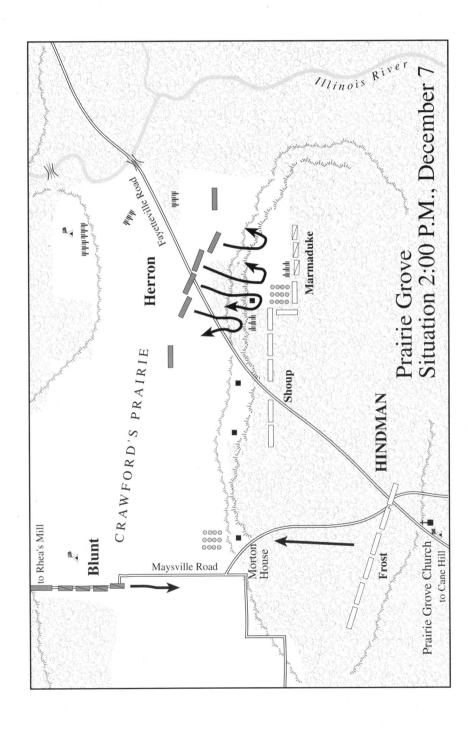

Prairie Grove
Situation 2:00 P.M., December 7

Illinois River

Fayetteville Road

Herron

CRAWFORD'S PRAIRIE

Blunt

to Rhea's Mill

Maysville Road

Morton House

Shoup

Marmaduke

HINDMAN

Frost

Prairie Grove Church

to Cane Hill

or abandoned, and the Confederate infantry and dismounted cavalry had taken cover on the reverse slope of the hill. The devastating barrage was another stunning demonstration of the superiority of Union artillery in the Trans-Mississippi.

When the Confederate batteries fell silent, Herron ordered two small Iowa and Wisconsin regiments forward—probably little more than 500 men. Herron clearly underestimated Confederate strength because he could not see through the foliage that blanketed the hill even in mid-winter. In truth, it may not have made much difference if Herron had known the actual situation, for he was a fighter, not a tactician.

The Federals advanced across Crawford's Prairie and up the wooded slope, easily overrunning an abandoned Rebel battery. They continued on past Archibald Borden's house and reached an orchard near the crest of the hill. There they were met by a furious counterattack and a "perfect hail storm of bullets" from Marmaduke's dismounted Arkansas and Missouri cavalry and Shoup's Arkansas infantry. "The orchard became a howling hell," wrote a shaken Iowa infantryman. Half of the Union soldiers were killed or wounded within minutes. The Confederates then advanced from three sides and drove the survivors back down the hill in disarray.

Wildly yelling Confederates, barely under the control of their officers, swept down the slope in pursuit. When they emerged from the cover of the trees onto Crawford's Prairie they were exposed to the Union cannon which had rolled forward to support the failed infantry attack. The Confederates were cut down in heaps by withering canister fire from the massed cannon at murderously close range. Panic-stricken survivors fled in confusion back up the hill.

That sight may have convinced Herron that the Rebels were broken, for he made the otherwise inexplicable decision to order a second attack over the same ground but with about the same number of men. Another pair of small regiments from Illinois and Indiana advanced across the prairie toward the tree-covered hill. "The whole woods was one continuous flash of fire," recalled an Indiana soldier. The Federals reached the crest, exchanged volleys for several minutes with vastly greater numbers of Confederates around the Borden house and orchard, then came tumbling back down. "As we came off the field the bullets were flying seemingly as thick as hail and nearly every one was struck either in his person or clothing," wrote another Indiana soldier. "I was one of three in my company who did not receive a mark of a bullet." Lieutenant Colonel John C. Black suffered a severely broken arm at the outset of the charge, but somehow led his 37th Illinois up the hill and back. His Medal of Honor matched that won by his brother at Pea Ridge nine months earlier. Such heroism did not disguise the fact that well over half of all Union casualties at Prairie Grove were incurred during these two senseless infantry assaults that never had a chance of success.

Despite the bloody repulse of the earlier Confederate pursuit across Crawford's Prairie, the failure of the

John C. Black: born Mississippi 1839; Black began his eventful Civil War career as a private in the 11th Indiana infantry in April 1861; he rose to sergeant major in the 11th before receiving a major's commission in the 37th Illinois Infantry in September; promoted to lieutenant colonel in July 1862; he performed with great distinction in the December 1862 Battle of Prairie Grove, Arkansas; severely wounded, he refused to leave the field until ordered to do so; promoted to colonel, Black served throughout the war, most notably as a brigade commander during General E.R.S. Canby's capture of Mobile in 1865, for which he was brevetted brigadier general of volunteers; in 1893 he was awarded the Medal of Honor for Prairie Grove; he served as commander in chief of the Grand Army of the Republic from 1903 to 1904; General Black died in 1915.

second Union infantry assault gave Hindman an opening. To this point only the Confederate right had been engaged, and the troops on that part of the field had clearly held their ground. Now Hindman had only to wheel forward his center and left and overwhelm Herron's decimated command. He could still win a decisive victory, but haste was essential, for Blunt would not tarry at Cane Hill after hearing the roar of battle to his rear. For reasons that are unclear, however, the Confederates west of the Fayetteville Road failed to threaten Herron's unsupported right flank. Then, in midafternoon, a huge cloud of dust approached rapidly from the northwest and artillery shells began to rain down on the Confederate left. Hindman's brief window of opportunity to defeat the Union army in detail had closed. Blunt's Division was on the field.

Blunt had passed most of the morning of December 7 at Cane Hill wondering why Hindman did not attack. He belatedly learned of suspicious Confederate movements east of his position during the night, then he heard the thunder of Herron's artillery in the direction of Fayetteville. Blunt realized at once that Hindman had gotten behind him and intercepted Herron. Furious at having been fooled, Blunt immediately marched his command toward the sound of the guns. It was fortunate for the Union cause in the Trans-Mississippi that he did so, for his troops arrived on the battlefield in the nick of time. Herron truly was in desperate straits.

Blunt did not take the most direct route to Prairie Grove despite the urgency of the situation. Rather than advance to the northeast on the Fayetteville Road, a route that led directly to the Confederate rear but would have made it impossible to cooperate with Herron, Blunt led his division north on a slightly roundabout route to Rhea's Mill where his train was located. After detaching a large cavalry force to safeguard the precious wagons and supplies, Blunt turned east and sent his troops rushing toward Prairie Grove in helter-skelter fashion.

Instead of toiling forward in column on the one available

road, the Federals surged toward the battle in a huge mass, each unit walking, trotting, or galloping forward across the open, rolling countryside at its own pace and on its own route. A few infantry regiments jogged almost the entire six miles at the double-quick, outpacing even some cavalry regiments. Among the first Union forces to arrive were several artillery batteries that rumbled onto Crawford's Prairie at full gallop and deployed for action in the most dramatic fashion possible. The gunners opened fire on the Confederate left to announce their presence. Herron's exhausted men responded with cheers and tears. Late in the afternoon Blunt's left and Herron's right made contact and thereafter the reunited Army of the Frontier presented a mile-long continuous front to the enemy.

Fighting at Prairie Grove now shifted to the area west of the Fayetteville Road, where Blunt's Division rapidly deployed opposite Frost's Division. Blunt brought another 4,500 men and three artillery batteries into the contest. The Confederates still held a slight numerical advantage, but not enough to make a difference, particularly with the strong Union advantage in artillery. Blunt, like Herron before him, did not hesitate to demonstrate his superior firepower. He unleashed his twenty-two cannon against the Confederate left and then advanced his infantry: five Kansas regiments, portions of two Indian Home Guard regiments, and one Iowa regiment borrowed from Herron's command.

Severe fighting erupted around the William Morton house at the base of the hill as the advancing Union soldiers clashed with Frost's Arkansas, Missouri, and Texas troops. The lines surged back and forth for an hour. Late in the day Frost gathered together all available reinforcements and launched a counterattack that pushed the Union troops off the hill and halfway across Crawford's Prairie. The Confederates sensed victory and swept down the slope in pursuit. Parson's Brigade of Missouri troops led the way. "We charged with a shout," Spencer Mitchell told his parents. "One of the enemy's batter-

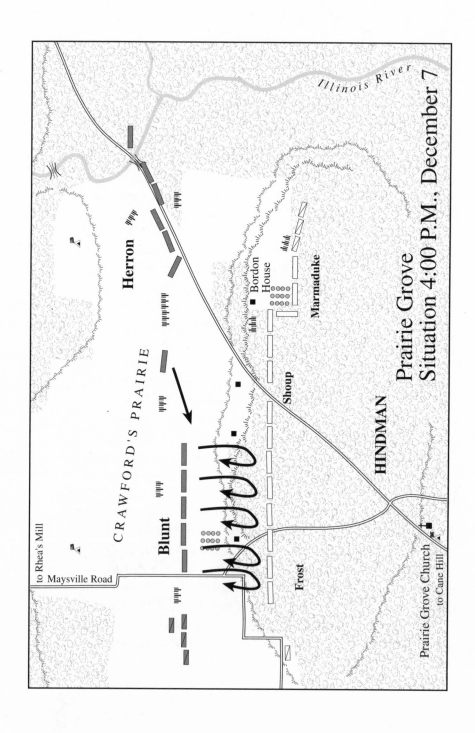

Prairie Grove
Situation 4:00 P.M., December 7

ies sent her infernal contents of grape and canister shot right into the midst of our regiment. The minnie balls of fifteen hundred muskets came whizzing around us. The sky was fairly darkened by the bullets, and for awhile the noise of musketry silenced that of the artillery. It was a terrible noise." Piles of dead and dying Confederates littered the grass in front of Blunt's line. The repulse of Frost's counterattack was a ghastly reprise of what had occurred a few hours earlier on Herron's part of the field. Surviving Confederates scrambled back up the wooded slope and remained there as darkness blanketed the field.

When the sun set around 5 P.M. it was obvious that neither army could dislodge the other. There were no more major assaults, though artillery fire and spasms of musketry sputtered along the lines until well after dark. Near the end of the battle haystacks and grass were set ablaze by sparks from the cannon and dozens of wounded soldiers from both armies burned to death.

During the night of December 7-8, Blunt ordered up 3,000 cavalrymen whom he had held in reserve at Rhea's Mill to guard his train. Hundreds of footsore stragglers from Herron's divisions limped in from Missouri. Hindman had no reserves to call upon and his stragglers either deserted or drifted back to Van Buren. Moreover, his artillery had been devastated and his men were low on ammunition. There was nothing to do but withdraw under cover of darkness.

Hindman realized that with the two armies so close together, a ruse would be necessary in order to effect a safe withdrawal. To deceive Blunt he requested a meeting under a flag of truce during the early morning hours of December 8. The two generals—one a fanatic secessionist, the other an equally committed abolitionist—dispensed with the usual courtesies of the era and addressed each other in surprisingly plain language. One Union observer gave the following account of the tense encounter.

Hindman: "Well I suppose General you give up."

Blunt: "Not by a d——- sight. I am ready to fight you in twenty minutes."

Hindman then proposed a cease-fire of thirty-six hours, ostensibly to retrieve the wounded and bury the dead, but actually to allow the First Corps to reach the safety of the Arkansas River valley. Blunt rejected the proposal.

Hindman: "I wish you to distinctly understand me General. I beg no favors."

Blunt: "Very well sir I will open on you in fifteen minutes."

Blunt and Hindman settled on a shorter cease-fire and parted without handshake, salute, or other ceremony. During the next few days they exchanged a series of increasingly sarcastic messages concerning the exchange of prisoners, burial of the dead, and other postbattle matters.

While Hindman bluffed and pretended to negotiate, the soldiers of the battered First Corps muffled the wheels of their artillery with blankets and quietly slipped away from the battlefield under the cover of darkness. They trudged back across the Boston Mountains and reached Van Buren on December 10, hungry, weary, and severely demoralized. Their dead and most of their wounded were left on the battlefield. Sometime during the day on December 8 Blunt learned that the Rebels had gotten away. He was outraged that Hindman had falsely proposed a cease-fire in order to cover his retreat, but comforted himself with the thought that the affair revealed the true nature of what he sardonically termed "southern chivalry." Blunt sent a courier galloping up Telegraph Road to let Curtis know that the Army of the Frontier had won a "complete victory" and that there was no danger of a Rebel resurgence atop the Ozark Plateau.

If Pea Ridge was a boxing match in which the combatants weaved and jabbed, Prairie Grove was a brutal slugging match in which the two armies traded direct frontal assaults until they were exhausted. Both sides claimed victory but in truth both sides lost. "For the forces engaged, there was no more stubborn fight and no greater casualties in any battle of the war than at Prairie Grove, Arkansas," declared Captain Henry E. Palmer of the 11th Kansas. Charles W. Walker of the 34th Arkansas agreed. He maintained that Prairie Grove "was not exceeded in fierceness and obstinacy by any battle west of the Mississippi." Sadly, both men were correct.

The toll for the one-day battle was severe. The Union Army of the Frontier went into battle with about 8,000 men and suffered 1,261 casualties: 175 killed, 813 wounded, and 263 missing. Most of the losses occurred in the terrible fighting around the Borden House on the Confederate right. Confederate numbers are problematic, as always. The First Corps brought roughly 11,000 men to the battlefield and suffered at least 1,500 casualties: over 200 killed, about 900 wounded, and upwards of 400 missing. In addition to men struck down in the battle, the Confederates also experienced serious desertion of conscripts during the campaign. Several hundred of these deserters, mostly northern Arkansans, changed sides after the battle and enrolled in Arkansas Union regiments. A reasonable conclusion is that each army lost over 15 percent of its troops engaged at Prairie Grove.

Pea Ridge is often said to have been the only major Civil War battle in which Indians played a role. In fact, a substantial number of Indians also participated at Prairie Grove. Blunt's Division included two Indian Home Guard Regiments, composed in large part of Creeks, Seminoles, and Cherokees (some of whom had fought on the Confederate side in the earlier battle). The Indians served primarily as skirmishers and flankers, because they preferred to fight from behind trees rather than stand in the open, and acquitted themselves well in this engagement.

9

THE FINAL ACT

In late December Blunt learned that Schofield had recovered his health and was on his way to resume command of the
Army of the Frontier. For several weeks Blunt and Herron had
toyed with the idea of a raid to the Arkansas River. They
believed that such an operation would disrupt the Confederate
logistical base at Fort Smith and make it impossible for
Hindman to launch another campaign in the foreseeable
future. The two generals feared that the ambitious but inept
Schofield would shoulder them aside and fritter away this
opportunity. Blunt decided to act while he still commanded the
Army of the Fronter.

On December 27 Blunt and Herron led 8,000 men—most of
the infantry, cavalry, and artillery in the Army of the
Frontier—on a rapid march across the Boston Mountains. The
Union soldiers made surprisingly good time on the primitive
roads that had caused the Confederates so much grief. The

cavalry, with Blunt riding very near the head of the column, stormed into Van Buren the next day, captured hundreds of surprised Rebels, and scattered hundreds more in all directions. The infantry followed later that day with a victory parade down Main Street. Bands played "Yankee Doodle" and soldiers sang "John Brown's Body." A Kansas soldier noticed that while most of the citizens were downcast, "the colored people seemed to enjoy it hugely." The Federals seized and burned three steamboats and a ferry, then burned a large warehouse along the riverfront filled with military stores. For good measure they ransacked business establishments and at least a few homes.

Hindman's battered command had suffered from wholesale desertions and a series of epidemics in the three weeks since the battle. He had only about 5,000 effective troops in the vicinity, most of them across the river from Van Buren in Fort Smith. He now regarded Blunt and Herron as formidable opponents and had no desire to tangle with them again so soon after Prairie Grove. In a fit of panic he needlessly burned two steamboats at Fort Smith and hastened down the south bank of the Arkansas River to Little Rock with what remained of the First Corps. The exodus was so abrupt that thousands of Confederate soldiers were left behind in Fort Smith hospitals. A disgusted Captain Ethan A. Pinnell of the 8th Missouri admitted that he and his fellow Rebels "took fright" and "skedadled in a manner, to say the least of it, that was decidedly unmilitary." Another great hue and cry was raised against Hindman in Arkansas, this time because of his military failures, and he was soon reassigned east of the Mississippi River.

Blunt had no intention of crossing the river to Fort Smith— he had no pontoon bridge and all available boats had been destroyed—and withdrew from Van Buren on December 29, his objective achieved. Accompanied by hundreds of liberated slaves and wagonloads of confiscated supplies, the Union column recrossed the Boston Mountains and returned to Prairie

Grove. Somewhere along the way Blunt and Herron met an unhappy Schofield, who later accused his two subordinates of hijacking and nearly ruining his army. As Blunt and Herron had feared, the Army of the Frontier soon was on its way back to Missouri, never to return to northwestern Arkansas. The Prairie Grove Campaign was over.

The course of events atop the Ozark Plateau during the fall and winter of 1862 was another severe blow to the Trans-Mississippi Confederacy. Hindman's First Corps fought Blunt's Army of the Frontier to a costly tactical draw at Prairie Grove, but the primary objectives of Hindman's offensive were to destroy Blunt's isolated division and recover northwestern Arkansas at the very least. Despite his promise to Holmes to return to Fort Smith, it seems likely that Hindman would have continued on into Missouri had he defeated Blunt. None of these objectives was achieved. The First Corps was wrecked and its men were dispirited. Prairie Grove was a dreadful affair for the Federals as well, but they succeeded in repulsing the Confederates and defending gains made earlier in the year. Missouri remained safely in Union hands and Confederate authority in Arkansas continued to atrophy.

"The war is over in Arkansas north of the river and in Missouri," wrote a Union officer at the close of 1862. Irregular warfare and cavalry raids would continue to exact a heavy toll in lives and property in both states, and in the Indian Territory as well, but the officer was essentially correct. Never again would major armies wind through the narrow canyons of the Boston Mountains or clash atop the scenic highlands of the Ozark Plateau. The repeated Union victories on the blood-soaked fields of northwestern Arkansas demonstrated the futility of continued Confederate efforts to reclaim Missouri.

The strategic importance of the Ozark Plateau declined after 1862. Union leaders shifted resources eastward to attack more vital points in other parts of the South, and embattled Confederate leaders did the same in order to defend them. The number of soldiers in the Trans-Mississippi steadily dwindled as veterans of Pea Ridge and Prairie Grove headed for other fields. Even as smoke still hung over Prairie Grove, huge campaigns were underway in Virginia, Tennessee, and along the Mississippi River that clearly demonstrated the future course of military and naval operations in the Civil War.

APPENDIX A
ORGANIZATION OF FEDERAL FORCES AT PEA RIDGE

ARMY OF THE SOUTHWEST
Brig. Gen. Samuel R. Curtis

FIRST AND SECOND DIVISIONS
Brig. Gen. Franz Sigel

FIRST DIVISION
Col. Peter J. Osterhaus

First Brigade
Col. Peter J. Osterhaus

25th Illinois, Col. William N. Coler
44th Illinois, Col. Charles Knobelsdorff
17th Missouri, Maj. August H. Poten
4th Independent Battery, Ohio Light Artillery, Capt. Louis Hoffman

Second Brigade
Col. Nicholas Greusel

36th Illinois, Col. Nicholas Greusel
12th Missouri, Maj. Hugo Wangelin
Welfley's Independent Battery, Missouri Light Artillery,
Capt. Martin Welfley

SECOND DIVISION
Brig. Gen. Alexander S. Asboth

First Brigade
Col. Frederick Schaefer

2d Missouri, Lt. Col. Bernard Laiboldt
15th Missouri, Col. Francis J. Joliat
1st Missouri Flying Battery, Capt. Gustavus M. Elbert
2d Independent Battery, Ohio Light Artillery, Lt. William B. Chapman

Not Brigaded
3d Missouri, Maj. Joseph Conrad
4th Missouri Cavalry (Fremont Hussars), Maj. Emeric Meszaros
5th Missouri Cavalry (Benton Hussars), Col. Joseph Nemett

THIRD DIVISION
COL. JEFFERSON C. DAVIS

First Brigade
COL. THOMAS PATTISON
8th Indiana, Col. Thomas P. Benton
18th Indiana, Lt. Col. Henry B. Washburn
22d Indiana, Lt. Col. John A. Hendricks
1st Battery Indiana Light Artillery, Capt. Martin Klauss

Second Brigade
COL. JULIUS WHITE
37th Illinois, Lt. Col. Myron S. Barnes
59th Illinois (formerly 9th Missouri), Lt. Col. Calvin H. Frederick
1st Missouri Cavalry, Col. Calvin M. Ellis
Battery A, 2d Illinois Light Artillery (Peoria Battery), Capt. Peter Davidson

FOURTH DIVISION
COL. EUGENE A. CARR

First Brigade
COL. GRENVILLE M. DODGE
4th Iowa, Lt. Col. John Galligan
35th Illinois, Col. Gustavus A. Smith
3d Illinois Cavalry, Maj. John McConnell
1st Independent Battery, Iowa Light Artillery, Capt. Junius A. Jones

Second Brigade
COL. WILLIAM VANDEVER
9th Iowa, Lt. Col. Francis J. Herron
25th Missouri (Phelps's Missouri Regiment), Col. John S. Phelps
3d Independent Battery, Iowa Light Artillery (Dubuque Battery), Capt. Mortimer M. Hayden

HEADQUARTERS UNITS
24th Missouri, Maj. Eli W. Weston
3d Iowa Cavalry, Col. Cyrus Bussey
Bowen's Missouri Cavalry Battalion, Maj. William D. Bowen

APPENDIX B
ORGANIZATION OF CONFEDERATE FORCES AT PEA RIDGE

ARMY OF THE WEST
MAJ. GEN. EARL VAN DORN

MCCULLOCH'S DIVISION
BRIG. GEN. BENJAMIN MCCULLOCH

Hébert's Brigade
COL. LOUIS HÉBERT
3d Louisiana, Maj. William F. Tunnard
4th Arkansas, Col. Evander McNair
14th Arkansas, Col. William Mitchell
15th Arkansas, Col. Dandridge McRae
16th Arkansas, Col. John F. Hill
17th Arkansas, Col. Frank A. Rector
1st Arkansas Mounted Rifles (dismounted), Col. Thomas J. Churchill
2d Arkansas Mounted Rifles (dismounted), Col. Benjamin T. Embry
4th Texas Cavalry Battalion (dismounted), Maj. John W. Whitfield

McIntosh's Brigade
BRIG. GEN. JAMES M. MCINTOSH
3d Texas Cavalry, Col Elkanah Greer
6th Texas Cavalry, Col. B. Warren Stone
9th Texas Cavalry, Col. William B. Sims
11th Texas Cavalry, Col. William C. Young
1st Arkansas Cavalry Battalion, Maj. William H. Brooks
1st Texas Cavalry Battalion, Maj. R. Phillip Crump

Artillery
Hart's Arkansas Battery, Capt. William Hart
Provence's Arkansas Battery, Capt. David Provence
Gaines's Arkansas Battery, Capt. James J. Gaines
Good's Texas Battery, Capt. John J. Good

Pike's Brigade
BRIG. GEN. ALBERT J. PIKE
1st Cherokee Mounted Rifles, Col. John Drew
2nd Cherokee Mounted Rifles, Col. Stand Watie
Welch's Texas Cavalry Squadron, Capt. Otis G. Welch

PRICE'S DIVISION
MAJ. GEN. STERLING PRICE

CONFEDERATE
First Missouri Brigade
COL. HENRY LITTLE
2d Missouri, Col. John Q. Burbridge
3d Missouri, Col. Benjamin A. Rives
Wade's Missouri Battery, Capt. William Wade
Clark's Missouri Battery, Capt. S. Churchill Clark
1st Missouri Cavalry, Col. Elijah Gates

Second Missouri Brigade
COL. WILLIAM Y. SLACK
Hughes's Missouri Battalion, Col. John T. Hughes
Bevier's Missouri Battalion, Maj. Robert S. Bevier
Rosser's Missouri Battalion, Col. Thomas H. Rosser
Landis's Missouri Battery, Capt. John C. Landis
Jackson's Missouri Battery, Capt. William Lucas
Riggins's Missouri Cavalry Battalion, Col. George W. Riggins

Third Missouri Brigade
COL. COLTON GREENE
Brigade not organized into units.

HEADQUARTERS UNITS
Cearnal's Missouri Cavalry Battalion, Lt. Col. James T. Cearnal

MISSOURI STATE GUARD

SECOND MSG DIVISION
BRIG. GEN. MARTIN E. GREEN
Division consisted of various skeletal infantry units.
Kneisley's Battery, Capt. James W. Kneisley

THIRD MSG DIVISION
COL. JOHN B. CLARK, JR.
1st Infantry, Maj. John F. Rucker
2d Infantry, Col. Congreve Jackson
3d Infantry, Maj. Robert R. Hutchinson
4th and 5th Infantry, Col. J. A. Poindexter
6th Infantry, Lt. Col. Quinton Peacher
Tull's Battery, Capt. Francis M. Tull

FIFTH MSG DIVISION
COL. JAMES P. SAUNDERS
Division consisted of various skeletal infantry units.
Kelly's Battery, Capt. Joseph Kelly

SIXTH MSG DIVISION
MAJ. D. HERNDON LINDSAY
Division consisted of various skeletal infantry units.
Gorham's Battery, Capt. James C. Gorham

SEVENTH AND NINTH MSG DIVISIONS
BRIG. GEN. DANIEL M. FROST
Divisions consisted of various skeletal infantry units.
Guibor's Battery, Capt. Henry Guibor
MacDonald's St. Louis Battery, Capt. Emmett MacDonald

EIGHTH MSG DIVISION
BRIG. GEN. JAMES S. RAINS
1st Infantry, Col. William H. Erwin
2d Infantry, Lt. Col. John P. Bowman
3d Infantry, Lt. Col. A. J. Pearcy
4th Infantry, Lt. Col. John M. Stemmons
Shelby's Cavalry Company, Capt. Joseph O. Shelby
Bledsoe's Battery, Lt. Charles W. Higgins

APPENDIX C
ORGANIZATION OF FEDERAL FORCES AT PRAIRIE GROVE

ARMY OF THE FRONTIER
BRIG. GEN. JOHN M. SCHOFIELD (ABSENT)
BRIG. GEN. JAMES G. BLUNT

FIRST DIVISION
BRIG. GEN. JAMES G. BLUNT

First Brigade
BRIG. GEN. FREDERICK SALOMON

9th Wisconsin, Lt. Col. Arthur Jacobi
6th Kansas Cavalry, Col. William R. Judson
9th Kansas Cavalry, Col. Edward Lynde
3d Wisconsin Cavalry, Maj. Elias A. Calkins
25th Battery, Ohio Light Artillery, Capt. Job B. Stockton

Second Brigade
COL. WILLIAM WEER

3d Indian Home Guard, Col. William A. Phillips
10th Kansas, Maj. Henry H. Williams
13th Kansas, Col. Thomas M. Bowen
1st Battery, Kansas Light Artillery, Lt. Marcus D. Tenney

Third Brigade
COL. WILLIAM F. CLOUD

1st Indian Home Guard, Lt. Col. Stephen H. Wattles
11th Kansas, Col. Thomas Ewing, Jr.
2d Kansas Cavalry, Lt. Col. Owen A. Bassett
2d Indiana Battery, Capt. John W. Rabb
2d Battery, Kansas Light Artillery, Lt. Elias S. Stover
3d Battery, Kansas Light Artillery (Trophy Battery),
Capt. Henry Hopkins

SECOND DIVISION
COL. DANIEL HUSTON, JR.

First Brigade
COL. JOHN G. CLARK
26th Indiana, Col. John G. Clark
7th Missouri Cavalry, Maj. Eliphalet Bredett
Battery A, 2nd Illinois Light Artillery (Peoria Battery),
Lt. Herman Borris

Second Brigade
COL. WILLIAM M. DYE
37th Illinois, Lt. Col. John C. Black
20th Iowa, Lt. Col. Joseph B. Leake
6th Missouri Cavalry, Maj. Samuel Montgomery
Battery F, 1st Missouri Light Artillery, Capt. David Murphy

THIRD DIVISION
BRIG. GEN. FRANCIS J. HERRON

First Brigade
LT. COL. HENRY BERTRAM
20th Wisconsin, Maj. Henry A. Starr
Battery L, 1st Missouri Light Artillery, Capt. Frank Backof

Second Brigade
COL. WILLIAM W. ORME
94th Illinois, Lt. Col. John McNulta
19th Iowa, Lt. Col. Samuel McFarland
Battery E, 1st Missouri Light Artillery, Lt. Joseph Foust

Cavalry Brigade
COL. DUDLEY WICKERSHAM
10th Illinois Cavalry, Lt. Col. James Stuart
1st Iowa Cavalry, Col. James O. Gower
8th Missouri Cavalry, Col. Washington F. Geiger
2d Wisconsin Cavalry, Maj. William H. Miller

Unattached Cavalry

1st Arkansas (Union) Cavalry, Col. M. LaRue Harrison

1st Missouri Cavalry, Maj. James M. Hubbard

14th Missouri State Militia Cavalry, Col. John M. Richardson

APPENDIX D
ORGANIZATION OF CONFEDERATE FORCES AT PRAIRIE GROVE

FIRST CORPS, ARMY OF THE TRANS-MISSISSIPPI
MAJ. GEN. THOMAS C. HINDMAN

ROANE'S DIVISION
BRIG. GEN. JOHN S. ROANE

Roane's Brigade
BRIG. GEN. JOHN S. ROANE

20th Texas Cavalry (dismounted), Col. Thomas C. Bass
22d Texas Cavalry (dismounted), Maj. Robert D. Stone
31st Texas Cavalry (dismounted), Lt. Col. George W. Guess
34th Texas Cavalry (dismounted), Col. Almerine M. Alexander
9th Missouri, Col. John B. Clark, Jr.
Reid's Arkansas Battery, Capt. James G. Reid
Shoup's Arkansas Battery, Capt. John C. Shoup

SHOUP'S DIVISION
BRIG. GEN FRANCIS A. SHOUP

Fagan's Brigade
BRIG. GEN. JAMES F. FAGAN

34th Arkansas, Col. William H. Brooks
35th Arkansas, Col. James P. King
37th Arkansas, Col. Joseph C. Pleasants
39th Arkansas, Col. Alexander T. Hawthorn
Chew's Arkansas Sharpshooter Battalion, Maj. Robert E. Chew
Blocher's Arkansas Battery, Capt. William D. Blocher

McRae's Brigade
COL. DANDRIDGE McRAE

26th Arkansas, Col. Asa S. Morgan
28th Arkansas, Col. John E. Glenn
30th Arkansas, Col. Archibald J. McNeill
32d Arkansas, Col. Charles L. Young
Woodruff's Arkansas Battery (Pulaski Battery),
Capt. John G. Marshall

FROST'S DIVISION
BRIG. GEN. DANIEL M. FROST

Parsons's Brigade
BRIG. GEN. MOSBY M. PARSONS
8th Missouri, Lt. Col. Charles Mitchell
10th Missouri, Col. Alexander E. Steen
11th Missouri, Col. DeWitt C. Hunter
12th Missouri, Lt. Col. William M. Ponder
16th Missouri, Col. Josiah H. Caldwell
Tilden's Missouri Battery, Capt. Charles B. Tilden

Shaver's Brigade
COL. ROBERT G. SHAVER
23d Arkansas, Col. Charles W. Adams
33d Arkansas, Col. Hiram L. Grinsted
38th Arkansas, Lt. Col. William C. Adams
Robert's Missouri Battery, Capt. Westley Roberts

MARMADUKE'S DIVISION
BRIG. GEN. JOHN S. MARMADUKE

Monroe's Brigade
COL. JOHN C. MONROE
Carroll's Arkansas Cavalry, Col. Charles A. Carroll
Monroe's Arkansas Cavalry, Lt. Col. Americus V. Reiff

Shelby's Brigade
COL. JOSEPH O. SHELBY
5th Missouri Cavalry, Lt. Col. B. Frank Gordon
6th Missouri Cavalry, Col. Gideon W. Thompson
12th Missouri Cavalry, Col. Beal G. Jeans
Elliott's Missouri Cavalry Battalion, Maj. Benjamin Elliott
Bledsoe's Missouri Battery, Capt. Joseph Bledsoe

MacDonald's Brigade
COL. EMMETT MACDONALD
MacDonald's Missouri Cavalry, Lt. Col. Merritt L. Young
1st Texas Partisan Rangers, Lt. Col. R. Phillip Crump
West's Arkansas Battery, Capt. Henry C. West

FURTHER READING

Anderson, Ephraim M. *Memoirs. Historical and Personal; Including the Campaigns of the First Missouri Confederate Brigade.* St. Louis, 1868.

Baxter, William. *Pea Ridge and Prairie Grove; or, Scenes and Incidents of the War in Arkansas.* Cincinnati, 1864.

Britton, Wiley. *Memoirs of the Rebellion on the Border, 1863.* Chicago, 1882.

Brooksher, William R. *Bloody Hill: The Civil War Battle of Wilson's Creek.* Washington: Brassey's, 1995.

Castel, Albert. *General Sterling Price and the Civil War in the West.* Baton Rouge: Louisiana State University Press, 1968.

Christ, Mark K., ed. *Rugged and Sublime: The Civil War in Arkansas.* Fayetteville: University of Arkansas Press, 1994.

Cutrer, Thomas W. *Ben McCulloch and the Frontier Military Tradition.* Chapel Hill: University of North Carolina Press, 1993.

Gaines, W. Craig. *The Confederate Cherokees: John Drew's Regiment of Mounted Rifles.* Baton Rouge: Louisiana State University Press, 1989.

Hartje, Robert G. *Van Dorn: The Life and Times of a Confederate General.* Nashville, TN: Vanderbilt University Press, 1967.

Josephy, Alvin M., Jr. *The Civil War in the American West.* New York: Vintage, 1991.

Monaghan, Jay. *Civil War on the Western Border, 1854-1865.* Boston, 1955.

Mullins, Michael A. *The Fremont Rifles: A History of the 37th Illinois Veteran Volunteer nfantry.* Wilmington, NC: Broadfoot, 1990.

Shea, William L., and Earl J. Hess. *Pea Ridge: Civil War Campaign in the West.* Chapel Hill: University of North Carolina Press, 1992.

Tilley, Nannie M., ed. *Federals on the Frontier: The Diary of Benjamin F. McIntyre, 1862–1864.* Austin: University of Texas Press, 1963.

Tucker, Philip T. *The South's Finest: The First Missouri Confederate Brigade From Pea Ridge to Vicksburg.* Shippensburg, PA: White Mane Publishing, 1993.

Watson, William. *Life in the Confederate Army.* New York, 1888.

PHOTO CREDITS

We acknowledge the cooperation of the U.S. Army Military History Institute at Carlisle Barracks, Pennsylvania for the photographs of Alexander S. Asboth, John C. Black, James G. Blunt, Eugene A. Carr, Samuel R. Curtis, Jefferson C. Davis, Daniel M. Frost, Francis J. Herron, Thomas C. Hindman, Theophilus H. Holmes, Benjamin McCulloch, John Sappington Marmaduke, Peter J. Osterhaus, Albert Pike, Sterling Price, John M. Schofield, Joseph O. Shelby, Philip Henry Sheridan, Franz Sigel, Earl Van Dorn, and Stand Watie.

The pictures of Elkhorn Tavern and the Battle of Pea Ridge, March 8, 1862, are from *Battles and Leaders of the Civil War.* I. (New York: Thomas Yoseloff, Inc., 1956).

INDEX